SELF-RENAISSANCE!

Inspirational Psychology for Self-Ecology!

Our Human Essence is in Self-Renaissance!

Rimaletta Ray, Ph.D.

WORKBOOK PRESS LLC
187 E Warm Springs Rd,
Suite B285, Las Vegas, NV 89119, USA

Website: https://workbookpress.com/
Hotline: 1-888-818-4856
Email: admin@workbookpress.com

Ordering Information:
Quantity sales.
Special discounts are available on quantity purchases by corporations, associations, and others.
For details, contact the publisher at the address above.

ISBN-13: 978-1-954753-75-4 (Paperback Version)
978-1-954753-76-1 (Digital Version)

REV. DATE: 20/10/2023

Acknowledgement

Rimaletta Ray, Ph.D. in Psycholinguistics from Riga, Latvia,, a published author of textbooks in the English language studies, currently working in the American Language Program of the University of Connecticut has now written her first book that ***puts psychology and the language in sync*** ,and frames her. poetic thoughts in the form of ***the universal spiritual, mental, emotional, and physical back-ups and inspirational mind-sets***, addressed to both native English speakers and second language learners.

Dr. Ray has forged a powerful message of hope and rejuvenation through effort, inner integrity, perseverance, and spirituality that touch the heart and the mind in the way music does. Her message is clear, "**Change yourself to change the world. Build up a strong Self-Renaissance Fort!**"

These poems are a true testimony to the indomitable human spirit which we all possess. What is unique in Dr. Ray's writing is her use of the language and her ability to guide the reader to think about the meaning of words. The visual spacing of them on the page and the breaks in the words enhance her writing, making the meaning more rhythmical, emotionally accessible, and very uplifting for everyone.

Whether read silently or aloud, these poems help us rediscover our written and spoken language with its nuances and its glory. Rimaletta's work reminds us of the voice within us all. She asks us to reach inside ourselves, pull our voices out, rejoice in our humanity, and spirituality, and lift our voices up! She holds us to a standard of belief, humanity, and action!

Poetry is in all of us! It is there when our children giggle and rhyme in a sing song and when we think our most basic thoughts...

This book returns us to the music inside each of us –

THE MUSIC OF THE SOUL!

Thank you, Dr. Ray!

Prof. Diane Rogers Montgomery

(UCONN , American Language Program , CT , 2005)

Epigraph

I'm Unique in Every Stance;

I was Born, but Only Once!

There Wasn't, there isn't,

There Won't Ever Be Anyone like Me!

Self-Renaissance of Being is My New Melody of Living!

I Choreograph My Life's Dance with Self-Renaissance!

Come into the Garden of My Soul to
Self-Console!

Come into the garden of my soul

That's the essence of my writer's goal.

My kindness is the ground,

My thoughts are the flowers,

My actions are the fruits,

My words are the roots.

I water it with inspiration

And root it off indifference and frustration.

Only then can I proceed

With the relaxation recede.

If you are ever alone

In the garden of your soul,

I invite you to mine

To be consoled.

So, share with me

Some of Thee!

My Goal is to Inspire Your Soul!

The Garden of My Soul is to Inspire and to Console!

(Isaac Levitan , The State Russian Museum, St. Petersburg)

Beauty is Me; Beauty is My Philosophy!

Inspirational Psychology for Self-Ecology!

SELF-RENAISSANCE = A HOLISTIC ACCULTURATION OF SELF!

Learn to be dynamic in expanding the World of Thought with a new Technological Tactic's Reward!

Use the Present-Day Technology to Maintain Your Self-Monitored Inner Ecology!

Contents

5. Time is Right to Accumulate New Personal Might!

6. <u>Personal Gravity Forms a Personality!</u>

7. Aristocracy of the EMOTIONAL DIPLOMACY

8. Mind is Logical, But Life is Not!

9. Become a Much Wiser Self-Actualizer!

10. So, Envision the Scenario of becoming a SELF-IMPRESARIO!

Everything is Possible if You Make Your Self-Renaissance Irreversible!

<u>Inspirational Psychology for Self-Ecology!</u>

(Book Rationale)

Life's Essence

is in

<u>Self-Renaissance!</u>

<u>"The Best Way to Predict Future is to Create it!"</u>

(Elon Musk)

(*See five books on Self-Resurrection that this book concludes in the physical, emotional, mental, spiritual, and universal circles of life. / www.language-fitness.com / Video -section Self-Resurrection*)

There's Nothing You Can't Do in Your
<u>New Life's Deja Vu!</u>

The Power of Now is in Your Everyday's
Life-Aware "WOW!"

(Isaac Levitan)

Synchronize Your New Life's Base with the Creator's Beautiful Haze!

1. Our Spiritual Salvation is in Inner Self-Emancipation!

Dear friends, the present-day mind-boggling reality of the exponential growth of technology changes **THE CONCEPT OF A BEAUTIFUL LIFE,** promoted by mass media and followed by us in an unconscious blindness about the enormity of this evolutionary change. "People lean to the dark side" *(David Wilcock)* But we are much more than the desire to have a beautiful mansion, an expensive car, and luxuries of all sorts. All these things can't exceed the self-worth - our main boss or the heart + mind based conscious living when we can **RIGHTFULLY** declare,

I'm Free to Be the Best of Me!

Time has changed, and every one of us, irrespective of the skin color, nationality, religious affiliation and financial status must launch **SELF-EMANCIPATION** from the old habits and beliefs or *"casting out demons"* that are still in the way of our Self-Resurrection to light and technologically enhanced Self-Creation. The time demands we change our limited, outdated, subjective consciousness to the objective, new knowledge-updated, evolutionary-enlightened **SELF-CONSCIOUSNESS.**

Let's sing the melody of life that's without any dogmatic self-strife!

We need to harmonize our lives and enact our yet dormant intuition + conscience direct line with the Universal Mind. Happiness, success, and prosperity cannot be obtained in the dependence on the society, the loved ones, or on God. *"The first indication of inner slavery is the absence of responsibility for your own life!"* *(Anton Chekhov)* Our life unawareness and lazy dependence on the circumstances are the regular pattens of complaining and life-blaming. We need to self-reform and put on a new, time-modified **SELF-CONSCIOUSNESS** uniform.

.Life-Gaining is in Self-Reframing!

2. We Are Here to Discover Ourselves!

Science has it that our intelligence and self-consciousness are part of the dynamic Universe and its **Universal Informational Field**. In other words, a human being is intellectually and spiritually channeled in life by the Universal Mind. Humanity is on a spiritual journey, the destination of which is the unification with God, or *"obtaining spiritualized intelligence which means uniting with the Divine."*

With the help of the self-inductively installed **AUTO-MEDIA**, or your personal Wi-Fi, a sharpened self-perception of the new reality and a new digitized **INTUITION + CONSCIENCE** link that constitutes the code of the heart + mind coherent support, we must enhance our immense creativity, expand *"spiritualized intelligence"*(Dr. Fred. Bell)and develop our digitally monitored self-consciousness. As *Gregg Braden* says, *"We are the product of simulation of an intentional virtual reality."* New ethical precepts are getting instilled in us now. **WOW**!

Self-Renaissance, therefore, is the process of a **CONSCIOUS SELF-SCULPTURING** that becomes urgent in view of the Technological Renaissance that is looming menacingly over us and that we must adjust to, regulate, and manage to our Self-Renaissance advantage.

Technological Renaissance leads to Self-Renaissance!

The religious paradigm that the humanity has been following for centuries has contributed a lot to our spiritual growth, but *we've come to the point of no return in it* because our religious differences are pushing our personal growth to stereotyped thinking, divisive judgment, and stagnation. It is paramount for us, therefore, to re-assess the reality with *spiritualized wisdom* that imbues us with *the Common Goal of a global dimension* to accomplish Renaissance nation by nation!

Be Strong in the Inner Fort; Learn to Be Godly in the Godless World!

3. Philosophy of Immediate Gratification Is Too Shallow for a Great Nation!

Unfortunately, the present-day life is re-framing us both technologically and personally, only to solidify the **Immediate Gratification Skills.** We can easily get in touch with anyone anywhere, set a date, or order whatever we need . It's great, on the one hand, but very destructive and addictive, on the other because *we get impulsive and technologically dependent, both mentally and emotionally.* Instant gratification pushes us away from personal growth, **affecting our mental sanity and emotional gravity.** Kids get acculturated not through books, classic music and art, but through apps and social media self-extensions that generate irritability when reality intervenes with their virtual world.

Young people are unwilling to think on their own. They would rather plagiarize their papers than display critical thinking skills. They have no *Emotional Intelligence (Daniel Goleman)* and therefore, they display no **EMOTIONAL DIPLOMACY SKILLS** needed to perform **mind-to-mind** and **heart-to-heart** communication that the globalization of economy demands from us exponentially now.

No Exceptional Individuality = No Self-Renaissance Modality!

Obviously, there's no *Self-Renaissance* without controlling our mental-emotional stance, *always, not once!* Fortunately, hundreds of people gather for TED talks and You Tube seminars to meet most advanced thinking and accomplished people. The question **HOW TO LIVE?** is also in the eyes of my life-confused students. So, my answer to their insightful minds, eager to validate their unique identity is:

To Physically, Emotionally, Mentally, Spiritually, and Universally Thrive,

Be Your Own Coach in Life!

4. *Self-Education* is Inseparable with *Technological Acculturation!*

However, personal evolution is often side-tracked or is totally neglected while it should be based on *the holistic awareness of the reality and Self* and backed up with the **SCIENCE OF LIFE.** "Science literacy" (*Dr. Neil deGrasse Tyson*) must be the backbone of our present-day education of self-formation that must be based on new life awareness, the *Emotional Diplomacy skills,* and the technological *Information Processing skills.* We also need to connect our impersonal, disconnected hearts and minds into new links of hearts and minds, not blinded by prejudices and religious dogmas. As. *Dr. Joe Dispenza* says,

"A new personality is a new personal reality."

Self-Renaissance is, therefore, the process of re-defining of the self-creation role in the present-day life and conscious channeling of it to full self-realization by the **KNOW-HOW** in the mind that is enhancing new, technologically based **SELF-ACCULTURATION.**

"We are here to be All we can be, not a fraction." (*Dan Pena*)

New, technologically enhanced acculturation will enable us to see life holistically and solve problems strategically, not just with the multi-tasking control that makes us "*Jacks of all trades and masters of none.*" With the *physical, emotional, mental, spiritual,* and *universal self-monitoring* of our lives, conducted with a breath-taking precision, modified by the Super Artificial Intelligence, we'll gain more self-knowledge (*physical level*), observe self-control and self-restriction (*emotional level*), focus on the enrichment of intelligence (*mental level*), have less self-justification and more faith (*spiritual realm*), and finally, achieve full self-realization (*universal realm*) of our mission on Earth.

(Rule # 1 of Self-Renaissance)

The Art of Living is the Art of Becoming!

5. Authenticate Your Unique Fate!

Thus, the aim of the book "*Self-Renaissance*" is to conclude the set of **5** books on Self-Creation, presented below and **2** more books on Love and Self-Worth, completing the *Paradigm of Self-Resurrection*, featured consequentially in the *physical, emotional, mental, spiritual, and universal* realms of life. We have developed technologically, but we remain savages in all these domains, anyway. Self-Renaissance means, therefore, not continuing to be what you've been but becoming what you Can Be! I'll focus here on the necessity to develop SELF-RENAISSANCE SKILLS, based on aware attention, problem solving and information processing skills because without them, human + technological evolution remains a problem, not a solution.

So, the book "Self-Renaissance" is the final synthesis of the holistic presentation of the concept. It encompasses my previous five books on Self-Resurrection, focused on the conceptual significance of each stage separately, but retaining the same structure in each book. Self-Renaissance is also viewed in the same dimensions (*physical, emotional mental, spiritual, and universal*), comprising the concluding stage of the Psycholinguistic Operational System of Self-Creation.

Levels:		Stages of Self-Resurrection:	Books ,featuring these stages:
5. *Universal level*		**Self-Salvation**	" *Beyond the Terrestrial!*"
4. *Spiritual* level		**Self-Realization**	" *Self-Taming!*"
3. *Mental level*		**Self-Installation**	*"Living Intelligence or the Art of Becoming"*
2. *Emotional level*		**Self-Monitoring**	" *Soul-Refining!*'
1. *Physical level*		**Self-Awareness**	" *I Am Free to Be the Best of Me!*"

The Holistic Methodology of Self-Creation, presented in these books is based on the concepts of order, technologically rationalized living, and *Emotional Diplomacy Skills,* central for our evolutionary growth.

Launch Yourself into the Technological Transformation of Your Life Holistically!

6. The Holistic Paradigm of Self-Creation

I've tested this **holistic paradigm of Self-Creation** with hundreds of my students who discovered their exceptionality, having instilled the **plan of action** in their minds. Their hunger for simple, digestible knowledge of life is amazing! I'm more than happy to watch them upload their smart phones with the mindsets from my books because the **inspirational, psychologically based and rhyming mind-sets** are easily memorized and are very motivational. *(www.language-fitness.com)*

With the plan of action, instilled in their vision, they uplift their spirit and enhance their desire to become advanced-thinking people with many great role-models to motivate them in the USA and in the world.

Seeing their elation and enthusiasm for the **KNOW-HOW** of Self-Resurrection *(See the link to the video)*, I realized that the initial paradigm had to be enriched with the book about love that is our main incentive in life and an enigma that confuses the young minds. This is how the book ***"The State of Love from the Above" / 2019,*** featuring five dimensions of love - *physical, emotional, mental, spiritual, and universal* came along. It was republished later as "**Love Ecology,** *2020.*

However, my further research brought me up to the idea to write the seventh book on self-creation, called **"Self-Worth"** because it became evident to me that unless a young person *identifies his exceptionality in life as his universal goal of self-realization*, granted to him / her from the Above, no blueprint of self-growth can actually work to its full potential. Otherwise, the students identify their goals in life only as connected to their future professional status and a good job, the choices often dictated by the demands of the market, not by the passion for a holistic self-realization. **Our personal force must be based on self-worth** that can be technologically enriched through self-education now.

A High Velocity of Self-Worth is Your Life's Holistic Course!

7. The Complete Blueprint of Self-Renaissance

So, the five stages of **Self-Resurrection** as presented in five books, listed above, are based on the idea of Self-Resurrection in the *physical, emotional, mental, spiritual, and universal* cycles of life to make a person realize that with **the plan of action** in the mind, he /she **has the resurrection power** that helped Jesus Christ to be raised to **His eternal Exceptionality**. Each of us needs to rise to his / her exceptionality, too, without any Ego, national, religious, racial, or material vanity!

Thus, the book **"Self-Renaissance"** has become the eighth book that is concluding the holistic **Self-Actualization Operational System**. I would like to draw the parallel here with the shape of our **DNA,** the double helix spiral of an unfolding number **8.** These eight books are meant to help you acquire the **GRAMMAR OF LIFE** holistically, preserving the spiral of the universal paradigm - **Synthesis** -**Analysis** – **Synthesis.** A much deeper awareness of the breakthroughs in different fields of knowledge and, especially in brain science, is needed now. The understanding of the brain at least at the dilettante level will help our students monitor their minds better. Also, education must be vertical and considerably enriched with the **SELF-EDUCATION** skills in five strata of life - *physical, emotional, mental, spiritual, and universal:*

1. our early *self-discovery* - **Self-Awareness;**

2. obtaining **Emotional Diplomacy** skills - **Self-Monitoring**;

3. gaining *professional maturation* - **Self-Installation;**

4. substantial raising *self-consciousness* - **Self-Realization;**

5. justifying *the goal of our existence* on Earth - **Self-Salvation.**

"The Life that is Not Structured is Not Worth Living!" (Socrates)

8. The Stages of Self-Renaissance Continuity

The train of continuity goes from simple to complex, from the microcosm to the macrocosm of Self-Development.

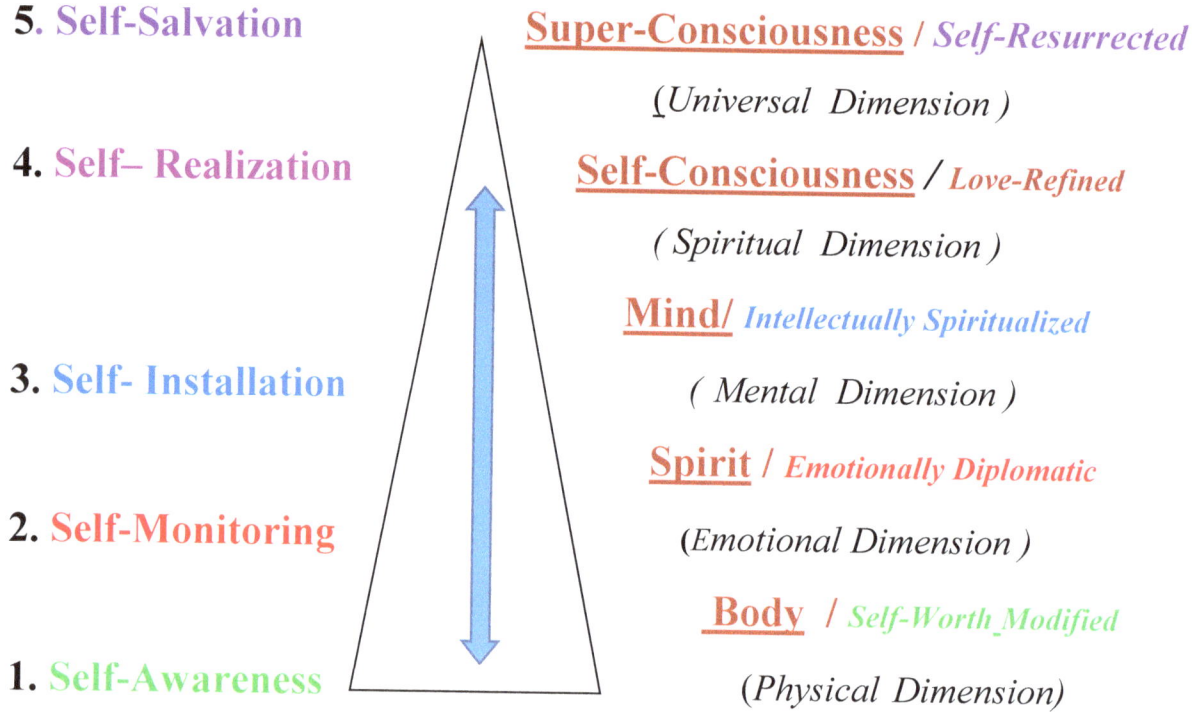

5. Self-Salvation   **Super-Consciousness** / *Self-Resurrected*

(Universal Dimension)

4. Self– Realization   **Self-Consciousness** / *Love-Refined*

(Spiritual Dimension)

Mind/ *Intellectually Spiritualized*

(Mental Dimension)

3. Self- Installation

Spirit / *Emotionally Diplomatic*

(Emotional Dimension)

2. Self-Monitoring

Body / *Self-Worth Modified*

1. Self-Awareness   *(Physical Dimension)*

The Holistic Paradigm of <u>five-dimensional Life-Renaissance</u> is the same in its core as that of ***Self-Resurrection***, presented in five books + three more books, including this one:

= Self-Ecology -Modified + **Emotionally Diplomatic** + Intellectually Spiritualized + Love -Refined + Self-Worth-Defined = Self-Renaissance -Obtained!

<u>Body + Spirit + Mind) + (Self-Consciousness + Universal Consciousness</u>)

Have the vision of this paradigm , *or its* <u>visual analogy,</u> *presented in eight books in your mind. You do not need to read them consequentially. Read them randomly, basing your choice on the needs that you might have in the* **physical, emotional, mental spiritual, universal** *circles of life. Each book is viewed through the prism, declared in the title as its main conceptual focus.*

1.”I'm Free to be the Best of Me!   *2.“Soul-Refining”*   *3.“Living Intelligence or the Art of Becoming!'*   *4.“Self-Taming!”*   *5.“Beyond the Terrestrial!”*   *6. “Love Ecology”*   *7. “Self-Worth “*   *8. “Self-Renaissance”* = A New You!

"Science is Organized Knowledge!"(Herbert Spencer)

9. Educational Gravity + Technological Sanity

In sum, the holistic system of self-education that I promote here proves that we need a new type of **EDUCATIONAL GRAVITATION** that translates into <u>a new holistically sustainable personal gravity,</u> based on the conscious *physical, emotional, mental spiritual, and universal* **ACCULTURATION** of a person. The problem is, we have not developed holistically at all, and the reality demands just that from us.

Only experiencing the magnetic force of the Mother Earth consciously, can we obtain the sense of **ONENESS** with everything and everyone around us. Like a rocket, launched into space needs to overcome the gravitational force of the Earth, we need to first accumulate ours to mentally fly beyond the terrestrial boundaries. ***"Reconditioning our thoughts and feelings, we bridge science and spirituality."*** *(Dr. Joe Dispenza)* Acting differently, we're becoming different personalities.

So, ***Self-Renaissance*** means becoming much better than you are by synchronizing oneself *physically, emotionally, mentally, spiritually, and universally.* The accumulation of **SELF-GRAVITY** relates to changing the thoughts and behaviors that are forming emotional sanity. Each of us needs to develop the sense of personal gravity as an **EMOTIONAL ANCHOR.** Such gravity is formed ONLY with the help of the **HOLISTIC SELF-EDUCATION** that is focused on life awareness + **NEW** information processing skills. *(See below)* Such education must also instill in the mind <u>Emotional Diplomacy and language fitness skills.</u>

The lack of emotional diplomacy in life is generated by ***the lack of personal gravity*** - the inability to ground the negative thoughts and emotions. Emotionally, we are under-developed savages, and the world can still be characterized with the famous words of *Carl Yung,* used by him to describe his visit to America.

We Live in the World of "Civilized Barbarism."

10. Let's Choreograph the Flow of the Civilization on the Go!

Concluding **Book Rationale**, let's not forget that the minds of the present-day young people are simplified by scanty reading, the virtual reality games, and the desire to just kill time and destroy their evolution-gained personality matrix. To come to terms with Self-Renaissance in life, **they need to be holistically alive!** Just this warning won't work:

Don't be in a hurry to live; life is not instant coffee!

True, Artificial Intelligence and our merging with it is overwhelming, but it's not the enemy. We need to integrate our biological world with the digital one (*the phenomenon of Singularity*) in **a new, consciously creative and regulative way**! Our reality is already monitored by the virtual copies of us out there. But we should not let our kids become total victims of it. We must holistically prepare them *to be conscious managers, makers, and regulators of hybrid beings.* However, the knowledge of the **HOW** to monitor the reality consciously is not there.

Life is universal in nature, and our skills to manage it must be directed toward **the universally objective standards** that will serve as an initial structure and take us far beyond the terrestrial boundaries in the future.

In short, as a concerned educator, I offer the **KNOW-HOW** for Self-Renaissance here as the science-backed up *holistic theory of the ways of conquering the passions of life consciously,* enacting not the penalties involved for not following the messages of God, but perceiving the new reality with new knowledge about life and Self. **"Scientific knowledge is the origin of our future consciousness!"** *(Elon Musk)* New knowledge will also synchronize us with the Universal Intelligence and humble us before we become too exalted. *"One who exalts himself first shall be humbled,"* for as *King Solomon* reminds us,

" It Too Shall Pass!" *(See the book "It Too Shall Pass!" / 2020)*

Drive through the Time and Space with the Self-Renaissance Goal on Your Interface!

(The Picture Collection of Fred Cronin)

To Establish a Personal Verizon, Outline Your Own Horizon!

Let's from the Beginning Sing Hymns to Living and Being!

(An Inspirational Preamble to stop the Unconscious Life-Gamble)

Whatever happened, remember, it was just a bad day, not a bad life!

Rule # 2 of Self-Renaissance)

Don't Be a Down-to-Earth Guy; Defy the Common Gravity - Fly!

There is No Self-Renaissance without Life-Reverence!

"Life is a miracle

that you can't be stopped with a sigh;

Long live the amplitude –

Either you fall or fly!"

(Edward Bagritsky in my translation)

Life is a fractal unity of the form and content of your life:

Form + Content

(Body+ Spirit+ Mind) + (Self-Consciousness + Universal Consciousness)

Living Intelligence + Enlightened Self-Consciousness = Self-Renaissance!

Remember, all pieces of advice that you've heard, self-help books, talks on self-transformation, etc. are just pieces of the puzzle, *but not the whole.* That's what your job is!

Self-Renaissance is getting

Soul-Reconstituted, Self-Consciousness Rebranded, Mind+ Heart United, and Self-Realization Ignited!

Rule # 3 of Self-Renaissance)

"Follow the Bliss" of the Uncatchable IS!

1. To Be One of the Best Life Cell - Conquer Yourself!

The world is full of unhappy people that seek to satisfy their internal hunger for the solution of their daily problems and get the answer to the question, "What am I here for?" To answer this question, we need to take the side of light in life and stay there, by charging ourselves with light *physically, emotionally, mentally and spiritually, and universally.*

We've all heard the statements" Live is not easy! Life is not fair!" Right! But the question is **WHY**? Do we have to blame life or ourselves? Till this day, we have no instruction how to live, and what the **KNOW-HOW** of the phenomenon, called **LIFE** is. We often hear complaints, curses, and whining. We still cannot wrap our minds around the idea to *consciously and knowingly* change the life ourselves.

The question "HOW DOES LIFE WORK? in general, and yours, in particular, must be our main incentive in life! The problem is, we lack **STRATIGIC PLAN OF ACTION**, or the blueprint of self-creation, on the one hand, and an individualized recipe for each disturbed soul, on the other. We need to sow new, holistic seeds in our life to thrive! Also, new knowledge must be consciously instilled in our minds. Just saying "I know"' is not enough now. "I'm aware of that" sounds more convincing. Unfortunately, most of us spend lives, bouncing back and forth between the good and evil of life. It wears us out and deplete us of the spirt for self-transformation, let alone for Self-Renaissance.

The present-day science has it that we can throw the Earth's hemostasis out of balance due to our *backward thinking and dissatisfaction with life.* Apparently, everyone needs much more **LIFE AWARENESS** and food for thought to feed the broken spirit with new knowledge. So, *the Law of Sow and Reap* must be the fundamental spiritual law of life-construction for us. Living consciously is the first rule of this Law!

Don't Take Life for granted. It's God-Granted!

2. Human Strife Must Be Absorbed by the Beauty of Life!

To begin with, we need to re-appreciate life and our place in it. The beauty of life doesn't stop to surprise us. We say, *" It's awesome!,"* but there is no awe in our actions because we take life for granted A pioneer of aviation *Igor Iv. Sikorsky* used to say, *"An ugly plane won't get off the ground."* A great Russian writer *Feodor Dostoevsky* wrote, *"Beauty will save the world." Nicolai Roerich*, enriched his words, saying *"Only consciously perceived beauty of life will save the world!"*

Meanwhile, we do not give conscious significance to life. The ugliness of our relationships, our social and personal life-strife, cheating, and mindless living pollute our emotional make-up and erode the souls. We don't have the *Emotional Diplomacy Skills* that are even more vital at the time of the fusion of the Artificial Intelligence and the mind of man, when the simulated reality is gradually becoming our main one.

The schools of gentlemen and ladies in Great Britain, France, and other most civilized countries have left the images of the best manners and records of diplomatic behavior in the history of the mankind. There was *the School of Nobility* for boys and girls in the pre-revolutionary Russia, too. The subjects, taught there - *etiquette, manners, and morals* were as important as mathematics, physics, and literature. Their rule was,

Don't be Life-Erratic or Life-Static; Be Life-Aristocratic!

Regrettably, our social life now is characterized with shamelessness, lack of morals, absence of manners, and a lot of profanity. We are aware of that, but we keep going down the road of self-corrode, blaming the society, the level of education, or the lack of money. Meanwhile, the best of us work on *"the extension of life beyond the Earth"* (*Elon Musk*).

Character-Ration is Our Nobility Formation!

Life is My Main Prayer!

(Best Photos -The Internet Collection)

My Admiration with it is Always There!

3. "Life is Just a Moment of Our Self-Solution."

The main messages of this book life-wise are: **To change your life, change yourself! Love life and it will love you back!** We live in the country of human inspiration and a new life formation! I have started the preamble to the book with the **PANEGYRIC** to a creative, self-realized life, the life of real doers, not complainers because I'd like to remind you of some very convincing words of some great thinkers that teach us to appreciate life and living, especially at the time of our technologically enhanced being.

" **Unhappiness is an unconscious living,**" (*Osho*)

"**Depression is a self-inflicted disease!**"(*Antony Robins*)

"***Don't get stuck in your past. You won't be there again.***" (*Muhammad Omar*)

Yes, so many times, joy is fleeting, and difficulties of life come roaring back.

*But let's remember the words, written by **Dr. G. I. Shipov**, an academician, a Noble Prize winner,* the scientist who discovered ***the torsion fields*** of energy that vibrationally envelope us everywhere. "*We live one life with the Universe. All the planets and the Sun itself are the living entities of a much higher intellectual and spiritual level than ours. **The Earth is our motherly planet that endures us as we endure the microbes in the body.** A man dies when his program on Earth is completed. By the special energy channels with which a man is connected to cosmos or **the Universal Intelligence**, he leaves his body in the form of transformed energy and goes to **the Archives** - the informational software of ideas in the space where all the information about our past and present lives is stored. **This world of ideas** is forming the World of Super Reality which we must be aware of to change ourselves. I don't know how this Superpower is made, but it is real.*"

(Rule # 4 of Self-Renaissance)

"The One who Found Himself in this Reality is like the Sun for his own Solar System!"

4. Lifetime = Self-Refine!

Lile is the light vibration

And matter formation!

As the building bricks of life,

We need to survive,

Orchestrating the vibration

Of our life's constant reformation.

Life, when it starts,

Is harmony and balance at once!

But we delete the cells' unity memo

With our thoughtless actions tremor.

We start with damaging the vibration of our speech

And gradually make our characters bewitched!

We choreograph an unconscious break-dance

Through twisting the conscience - not once!

We learn to live in dissonance

With the loved ones!

The disharmony of the hearts and minds

Becomes chronic and un-defined!

We adjust to its false tune

And stop being immune

To lying and yelling,

To cheating, fighting, and repelling!

So, what was the matter of the wrong course,

Becomes the matter, of course!

We also get used

To being often abused

For the religion, skin color, nationality,

Or the lack of personal vanity!

Finally, we lose identity

Of an individuality!

Life becomes grey,

And all the ambitious goals begin to sway.

Our personal vibration

Turns into a de-formation

And if we don't break free of its chains,

Life will end up without any gains!

On the steps of life, we can thrive in elation

Only if we fix our broken vibration!

So, be a Self-Boss! Put your distress with life in a reverse!

*In Japan, there is an incredible method **to rid a person of depression and life-negligence.** They simulate electronically a person's stay in the coffin, recording all the desperation and helplessness that a person experiences in that confinement. The recording is then given to the patient to be used instead of any anti-depressant.*

(Rule # 5 of Self-Renaissance)

Live with Zest! Life is Abreast!

5. Emotional Diplomacy Awareness

Life is a polar thing, consisting of happiness and joy, on the one hand, and suffering and sorrow, on the other. It is only natural because the universe is pulsating in frequencies of the ups and downs, with our hearts beating in unison - 21-21-21... The book *"The Power of Now"* by *Eckhart Toole* has awakened us to the present moment that is always new, teaching us to be conscious of the true rhythm of life and take both our failures and successes as the irreversible rule of the life game. ***Being conscious means being reasonably rooted in the reality!***

Our role in the life game is to bring the scales to the neutral position of inner equilibrium with the help of the **EMOTIONAL DIPLOMACY SKILLS** that must be developed in kids as early as possible because they are the ones who will become the" ***multi-planetary species."*** (*Elon Musk*). Kids must be brought up emotionally acculturated!

It means we must develop in them the ability to act with acute awareness and self-responsibility, with full realization of the logic of ***the Cause-Effect*** cosmic rule. It is the reflection of our impulsive and therefore, destructive, or **conscious** and therefore, **constructive** thoughts, feelings, words, and actions. Holistic and conscious self-growth is the only way to the emotionally diplomatic **SELF-ACCULTURATION** and life admiration.

Every day is a touch of faith and a work of Art, so to say!

Each moment is recorded in our emotions. *"**If we bring awareness into any negative emotion that we experience, we'll make them disappear."** (Dr. Jon Kabat Zinn)*. Dr. Karat Zinn also teaches us to view life with ***"the beginner's mind"*** in any new episode of life, bringing awareness to any activity of life - breathing, speaking, eating, driving, reading, or thriving. He calls it ***"non-judgmental awareness "*** or true mindfulness,

"Mindfulness is a Love Affair with Life."

6. The Trajectory of Self-Renaissance

The holistic paradigm that I introduce here will help you form the **HOLISTIC SELF-IMAGE** in five dimensions, and it must become <u>the main incentive for your Self-Renaissance</u>. I have outlined the first two steps *(the initial synthesis and the analysis of its formation above)*. When you come to the final ***Self-Synthesis,*** your holistic ***"The Best of Me!"*** self-image will be constructed in the mind. I am sure that you have taken this book into your hands because ***you know that you are very special,*** but you have not yet arrived at the point. The holistic paradigm has helped many of my students become ***charismatic, outspoken, and personable.*** No one holds a good opinion of a man who has a low opinion of himself, but <u>all of us need to justify our exceptionality!</u>

You must look at yourself as a vantage point of eternity.

However, the feeling of self-acceptance is not instilled in our emotional and mental make-up overnight. To conduct the most **OBJECTIVE** <u>Self-Renaissance scanning</u> in five levels - ***physical, emotional, mental, spiritual, and universal***, you must perform a thorough <u>selection and organization</u> of the good and bad qualities that you have. The next two chunks of information present the examples of the two pyramids of constructive and destructive character traits that might be helpful.

I suggest you compare *"The Best of Me!"* and *"The Worst of Me!"* pyramids below as the positive and negative holistic images of yourself, Work out a holistic, objective + / - <u>visual image of yourself.</u> as a back-up for a consciously monitored Self-Renaissance. During your goal-oriented self-creation *(See the video, section Self-Resurrection)*, cross out the weaknesses on the negative pyramid and add into the empty spaces the positive traits of character that you've managed to develop. ***It will be the trajectory of your technologically enhanced Self-Installation.***

Choreograph Yourself to Self-Excel!

7. "The Best of Me!" Self-Image

To begin with, focus on the holistic **"The Best of Me! self-image -** <u>a human being with his own mind, his own timing, and his own creative agenda.</u> Take a look at the piramid of some major self-constructive personality traits, presented in five dimensions. A common tool for analysing character strengths is holistic <u>Self-Scanning</u>. I hope this chart will help you identify which strengths you can link your Self-Renaissance to. <u>Go from top to bottom.</u>

Universal Dimension

HIGH SELF-CONSCIOUSNESS, an altruist, intuitive, appreciative, giving, reliable, evil-resisting ,beauty-embracing, information-sensitive, very spiritual, super-conscious , having self-transcendence, enjoying life , . etc.

Spiritual , Dimension

Godly, spiritual, evil -fighter, conscientious, respectful loving, caring, empathetic, intuitive, compassionate, kind, fair, having humility, having cultural and social intelligence, heart and mind in synch, forgiving, selfless , subconscious-controlling, etc.

Mental Dimension

Intelligent, knowledgeable, interested, receptive to new ideas, cooperative , good judgement, demonstrating financi

having originality of thinking , creative, assertive, with leadership skills, realistic, having intelligence, conscious, etc.

Emotional Dimension

Emotional stability, language-taming, communicative, sympathetic, sensitive, taming anger, indifference, controlling

positive , respectful, agreeable, reserved cooperative, friendly ,helpful, responsive, sex drive, showing class, self-confident, etc.

Physical Dimension

Good health habits, high self-esteem, modesty , honesty, reliability, zest, smiley with inner beauty , considerate , displaying

industriousness, perseverance, self-efficacy, having responsibility, exuding love , shining self-respect , self-restriction, discipline. etc.

I'm a Free Me; I'm the Best I could Ever Be!

8. *"The Worst of Me" Self-Image*

Now, while doing the **Self-Analysis**, look at pyramid of the <u>self-destructive character traits</u> that you do not want to have on the path of implementing your Self-Renaissance. The banal statement, *"No one is perfect!"* is just a justification. Don't avoid people who criticize you and be sure to see where you are imperfect yourself. **We better grow on the negative flow!**

<u>We are on the spiral of life conquering evil inside!</u>

Universal *Dimension*

Ignorant spiritually, not an altruist, discontent with life and himself, grumpy,   *disconnected from the Source, very unhappy, wasteful in self-exceptionality , etc.*

Spiritual *Dimension*

Godless, cheating, dishonest, sinful, and social conditioning, constant interne ,vindictive , not consciensious, selfish,   *no moral intelligence, contaminated by cultural conflict, driven by his pattered behaviors, unkind unable to love, etc.*

Mental *Dimension*

Poorly educated, hardly ever reading, nobleness, inconsiderate, bossy, selfish, unconsciuous behaviors , ignorant,   *intellectually lazy, authoritative,no fairness, no chasing money, unwilling to think ahead, stubbon, limited,etc.*

Emotiona *Dimension*

emotionally unstable, moody, grumpy, ,anxious, doubtful ,reactive, often angry behaviors, disrespectful, indifferent,   *impulsive, fearful, aggressive, abusive ,conflicting prone to infidelity, displays attitude, risky sexual rarely smiles, untamed mouth, etc.*

Physical *Dimension*

Bad health habits, gluttony, low self-esteen, risky behaviors, smoking, substance abuse, poor diet, no perseverance, selfishness, disconunt , bad moods, dominant, grumpy, dissatisfied, no financial intelligence, bad manners,   vanity, anger, fear , hate, unforgiveness etc.---

"Bad Habits Have a Good Tendency-

<u>*Either You Kill them, or They Kill You!"*</u> *(A. Einstein)*

9. To Make Self-Renaissance Irreversible, Be Godly-Personable!

Next, let's look at someone who seems to be almost perfect, the people who possess **the characteristics beyond the conventional thinking,** with godly traits of character, love for life and "spiritualized intelligence".

It will be easier for you **to visualize and draw the pyramid of Self-Renaissance** that you would like to ascend.. I am sure you have met people like that at least once in your life. These people are called *luminaries, or sages* because they have high self-consciousness and illuminate our lives with their charisma and wisdom. Don't expect the message of repentance come from them. It must come from you!

The best of us have gone through a narrow passage to shape themselves.

1. They live in the bliss of what life Is! They are rational, conscious, life aware.

2. They are wise; they are intellectually spiritualized!

3. Their spirituality is real, and it is connected to the Universal Intelligence. It spreads to everyone and everything: nature, animals, every living being on earth.

4. Their perception of the world goes beyond the skin color, nationalities, and religious preferences.

5. Love is their guide; it is in their genes.

6. They are creators, but they are not materialistic. They are self-content and self-sufficient.

7. Their eyes are shiny, their voice is soft, their character is gentle.

8. Their thinking is slow, but very precise. They do not impose it on anyone.

9. Their language is respectful, controlled, sincere, exact. They say what they mean, and they mean what they say! Honesty is their policy.

10. They exude inner balance, tranquility, and emotional equilibrium.

11. They never lose their identity! They know who they are!

Let's Change the Melody of Life to Thrive, to Thrive!

10. Be Soul-Refining! Internalize and Externalize Your Becoming!

Science starts realizing that to change our **COMMON LIFE ON EARTH,** *we need to perform self-attunement to the Universal Intelligence - God.* Developing our conscious mind in synch with the sub-conscious one, we are developing **SUPER-CONSCIOUSNESS** or super-perception that makes it possible for us <u>to tune the mind and heart to the Super Mind</u> that is governing all life in the Universe. The Super-Mind releases the information that we tap into, and we need to learn to decipher it. When I write about **AUTO-MEDIA,** I mean the ability that some most spiritually advanced people already have. They tune to the higher vibrations, being literally enlightened by them when they perform channeling or generate new ideas in that connection.

Their vibrations are our navigating insights!

The Super-Conscious mind works with us on the sub-conscious level too, but to be able <u>to tune to its massages and reason them out</u>, we need to become more conscious, more spiritually-intelligent, and much more perceptive of the information that is being transmitted to us from the Above. **That's why our conscious living in the Now is so important!** Finally, every one of us is forming <u>a life fractal</u> *(see above),* topped by **SELF-CONSCIOUSNESS -** *the highest level of self-awareness, self-reflection, and spiritual maturity.* But only the most intelligent, conscious, and soul-refined of us have developed it so far. Such intellectually spiritualized people are being helped by the Universal Consciousness and merge with it in the outcome. The necessity to develop oneself holistically is, in fact, the process of developing such super-consciousness - <u>the goal of our life on Earth.</u>

(Rule # 6 of Self-Renaissance)

To Life-Thrive, You Need to Self-Derive!

11. Self-Quest is a Self-Renaissance Fest!

In sum, being focused, consciously and self-inductively channeled by **AWARE ATTENTION** is the route of mastering Emotional Diplomacy and boosting the time-demanding Self-Renaissance.. *Being the best is a tough test!* We need to take it to become self-elated, self-regulated, and Self-Resurrected! With the godly power that resurrects life, we must overcome the dark forces that break the heart + mind link and set **up** a new digital sync with the Universal Mind .

There are very many *left-brained people* now that are good at analyzing and detailing, but who lack the ability to systematize and generalize the information. That's why we have a lot of managers, but very few leaders who can *"tame the chaos" (Ravi. P. S .Berg)* in our heads and hearts and declare the power of the conscious mind over the sub-conscious one. Science has it that the conscious mind controls only *5 %* of the brain, while **95%** of it is controlled by the sub-conscious mind. I suggest using the rhyming **AUTO-SUGGESTIVE** programming *(See Part Two below)*to become a Self-Renaissance guru able to instill in the mind   conscious self-management, too.

Thus, to create an emotionally diplomatic personality, you must empower the sub-conscious mind that has an enormous creative power. To be holistically alive means to be unconsciously conscious! It will inevitably happen once you start controlling your sub-conscious mind consciously with the help of the Auto-Suggestive Psychology for Self-Ecology. So, to be self-refining, *generalize, internalize and externalize* your new, technologically monitored becoming

SELF-INNOVATION must become AN OBLIGATION!

We're Rewinding the Double Helix of our Animal DNA into the Five-Dimensional "Star People's Display!" (John Banes)

New Times = New Goals-Ascending!

(Isaac Levitan)

Ordain the Stairway of Your Life's Roles
with the Self-Renaissance Goals!

The Holistic Structure of the Book

(Synthesis - Analysis - Synthesis book formation)

There is No System

Without

the Structure!

*There is an urgent need for us to develop <u>aware attention to the reality holistically</u>, at each level of self-development, presented above **as the strategic plan of action**. Each level builds up on the one before, taking you a step further on the path of expanding your range of possibilities. Gradually, **thought will overpower emotion** and let you be in total charge of your evolving mind, heading toward "**TRANSHUMANISM**" (Ray Kurzweil) It should be a clearly visualized, well-disciplined, and a **SELF- MONITORED** process.*

Let's Explore Our Godly Essence of Self-Renaissance!

1. Anything that Happens Consistently Gets Linked!

The holistic awareness of how our life gets processed in time and space becomes an urgent necessity now. That's why I create the Self-Creation mode by which we can be consciously steering ourselves to full **SELF-ACTUALIZATION** in sync with the demands of our time. There are many great ancient philosophies, starting with the Hermetic and Kabalistic ones, that educate us how to move up *the Tree of Knowledge* to complete our spiritual mission as a valuable leaf of *the Tree of Life.* The question is how to apply all godly knowledge now. **Being godly is a new challenge in a technologically enhanced world!**

The magic of the present-day life demands that we re-program our brains without vanity, **from religiousness to spirituality** and evolve ourselves in sync with a new life perception. All sacred books teach us the universal wisdom. *"If we achieve the change of consciousness, we'll be able to enlighten the dark corridors of our lives."* (Rev. P.S. Berg) It's all true, and the **KNOW-HOW** of it must be modified for the needs of our digitized intelligence in a holistic and systemic way.

Just praying and church attending is not enough now!

The old framework of life is outdated. Our perception has changed over the centuries, and *our consciousness now should be synchronized with the demands of the digital technology* that is merging with the Artificial Intelligence. We are developing new standards of life, and we need to adjust our Three of Knowledge to the new reality. Each of us has his own *Tree of Knowledge*, which is our belief system that changes irreversibly, putting our lives into a new mold, shaped by the Universal Consciousness and our *intellectually spiritualized fractal formation*.

Unify Yourself and Reason Up from There!

2. Life-Manual and Self-Acculturation

It's important to visualize each stage of the paradigm as the **LIFE MANUAL**, illustrating *five stages of Self-Resurrection* below. See it as the cycles of the DNA spirals of your *"spiritually intellectualized"* and ***technologically enhanced fractal formation..*** The train of continuity goes from simple to complex or from the microcosm to the macrocosm. Self-Ecology is in Action-Taking and Life-Making!

5. Self-Salvation	*Universal Level-*	**Super-Consciousness**
4. Self– Realization	*Spiritual Level*	**Self-Consciousness**
3. Self-Installation	*Mental Level*	**Mind**
2. Self- Monitoring	*Emotional Level*	**Spirit**
1. Self-Awareness	*Physical Level*	**Body**

(Body + Spirit + Mind) + (Self-Consciousness + Universal Consciousness)

Anything that happens consistently gets linked!

Self-Ecology + Love Ecology + Self-Worth + Self-Renaissance =

(5 books+ 3 books) = AN ACCULTURATED PERSONALITY!

Unfortunately, ***our being determines our self-consciousness now*** while it should be the other way around.

Our self-consciousness must determine our being!

We all must ***raise the level of our self-consciousness*** in the *physical, emotional, mental, spiritual, and universal strata* of life because the avalanche of information that we get is transforming our consciousness now, and we need to consciously and knowingly monitor this process.

These are the Stages of Self-Acculturation for Self-Renaissance Formation.

3. Clarity and Orderly Consistency

Unfortunately,our educational system does not yet provide time-demanding **LIFE MONITORING + INFORMATION MANAGING SKILLS** that must be backed up with solid **Emotional Diplomacy Skills.** The minds of our young people lack the essential vistas of intelligence that the present-day reality demands to sustain the world of competition and to develop into technologically and consciously advanced personalities.*(See thee Excellence Book Award winner " Living Intelligence or the Art of Becoming!"/ mental dimension, 2020).*

Our memory links need thorough cleansing for the valid information to prepare an **INDIVIDUAL MIND** *physically, emotionally, mentally, spiritually, and universally* for the life in the new reality in which Self-Renaissance is a priority and realizing one's exceptionality is a goal!

Exceptionality can be discovered only in an individuality!

The new technologically exponential times demand that we fill up our minds with the exponential intelligence, *(ten essential levels of intelligence / See* ***Stage Three*** *below)* with the help of technologically enhanced insightful **SELF-EDUCATION.** Getting new, scientifically verified knowledge and developing the *Emotional Diplomacy Skills* is the way to a new **ACCULTURATION OF A PERSONALITY**. The rapid development of Super Artificial Intelligence obligates us to speed-up this process. So, we also need to develop a new level of *personal maturation,* based on exponential development of self-consciousness.

This is a huge task that can't be described in its entirety. I just generalize here my vision of the problem, trying to be consistent in its presentation in five circles of life in every book, mentioned so far, sticking to the holistic paradigm - *Synthesis – Analysis – Synthesis* that monitors our life at large. My academic experience is the proof of its validity.

Life-Elation is in Self-Education!

4. Synthesis – Analysis – Synthesis!

I have indicated above that the **Holistic Paradigm of Self-Creation** is presented initially in five books, featuring *physical, emotional ,mental, spiritual, and universal realms* of Self-Resurrection consequentially. I've structured these five books and two more, featuring **love ecology and self-worth** accumulation on the philosophic paradigm, analyzed in its entirety by *Dr Sam Gazarkh* as <u>System- Analysis -System</u>. This paradigm is the backbone of my entire system of Self- Creation - *8 books that can be read randomly, depending on the needs you have on this path.*

Each of us writes **his / her own book of life**, chapter by chapter. Each book has <u>the starting point</u> at birth. *(Synthesis)* Then a person is processing his life *(Analysis)* through its plot development around many conflicts between life and death, energy and entropy, good and evil, following the same holistic paradigm. <u>The culminating point</u> comes in the middle of the life story with the resolution of the conflict inevitably coming next, and, finally, a person rounds off his life story with *the conclusion* of the life cycle.*(Synthesis)*

The Catharsis, or the realization of the outcome of life, is to be experienced by each of us, too, and this is **the main conscious stage of our lives** that comes with the last breath of either gratitude or regret. We are all yarning for life contentment, for more self-recognition, for something that our souls long for, for full Self-Realization.

But we must <u>reject a lot of ignorance</u> that puts our self-consciousness out of its conceptual form. As *Leo Vygotsky* writes, "**We develop the soul and the spirit forces through only a well-educated, self-made man, able to accomplish full self-realization and become a personality**." Only by establishing order in our inside and outside worlds can we obtain such rewards.

The Universal Orderliness is Ruling the Mind's Mess!

5. Psychology and Language in Sync Form the Self-Renaissance Link!

In sum, I do not only declare the paradigm Synthesis -Analysis - Synthesis in every book of mine; I stick to it in the structure of every book *(See below)* because I think that our present-day presentation and processing of information should be changed in its structure.Time is gliding fast away, and we cannot waste time reading pages of extended information with the point hardly discovered in one paragraph. So, in this book, I present only *page-long chunks of information* with the rhyming titles that synthesize the declared concept, analyze it in the body part, and synthesize the information again with the rhyming mind-set at the bottom of the page. It is a concise, easily digestible, and technologically friendly shot-cut to the brain. Thus, I try to justify my background of a psycholinguist - Psychology + Language link in the rhyming philosophical sync.

Part One of the Book -*(Introductory opus with the philosophical focus -* **Initial Synthesis** *(The presentation of the theory of Self-Renaissance)*

Part Two of the Book – *Auto-Suggestive Psychology for Self-Ecology* – **Analysis** (*The Know- How of my Inspirational WOW!)*

Part Three of the Book –-*The Illustrative Part -* **Final Synthesis**

Part Three is **an inclusive part**. *It presents a general overview of the theory **in five stages of Self-Renaissance**, as the proof of the pudding - <u>universal, spiritual, mental, emotional, and physical</u> levels, illustrated from top to bottom:*

Self-Salvation - **Self-Realization** - **Self-Installation** -**Self-Monitoring** and **Self-Awareness.**

With a Clear-Cut Route in the Mind, Start Getting Holistically Soul-Refined!

Grow the Self-Renaissance Wings!

(Best Photos - The Internet Collection)

Self-Reflection is Self-Renaissance in Retrospection!

Part One of the Book

(Synthesis - Analysis - Synthesis structure of the book)

Technological

Acculturation

of a

Personality

What do we make of this rule now?

"Whoever commits a sin is a slave of sin"(John 8:34)

(Rule # 7 of Self-Renaissance)

Make Technology Work for Your Self-Ecology!

(Adjusting to the New Reality)

Technologically Enhanced Self-Worth Creates a New Self-Universe!

"A sufficiently advanced technology is indistinguishable from magic" (Arthur C. Clarke)

What is the rim of the technological sin?

It's not Just a Mental Shift. It's a Planetary Shift, and we are in its Evolutionary Drift!

1. Wow, We Live Now!

The cutting-edge of the exponentially growing, mind-blowing technology requires our **fast and qualitative self-creation**, too. At the time of the technological use of *the mixed reality and the possibility to produce an exact holographic and hybrid replica of a human being*, we remain inwardly *"in the stone age" (David Icke)*, still living unconsciously and being driven by our untamed emotions.

Our inability to forestall compromise, ground the desire to please, stand strong against an offender, and resist temptations is blocking the inner freedom and *the creativity of Elon Musk type* that helps us define ourselves differently in view of **the looming technological supremacy.** We must speed up and regulate the process of our technological **Self-Acculturation with conscious elation!**

The pursuit of knowledge, emotional control, and a dedicatedly realized exceptionality remain the pillars of **SELF-RENAISSANCE** that enlightened the humanity with **the first Renaissance** - the boom of the mesmerizing ideas in art and science in the 15th century. The beginning of the 20ieth century with its ground-breaking *Theory of Relativity* of *Albert Einstein ("the miracle year "of 2005)* and the mind-boggling technological innovations of another *super-genius, Nikola Tesla*, enriched the world with great discoveries in the macro and micro worlds that enlightened the world with the Internet and other miracles later.

That was the time of **the Second Renaissance** that culminated into *the digital revolution,* ruling our lives now. The process of information processing and its fundamental enrichment with the latest developments in science, or *mega-science,* has changed the scene of today's brutally competitive world that commits us to self-creation, too.

Whatever We Are, We Create!

2. The Third Renaissance is Digital Renaissance!

As a matter of fact, our time now is the time of <u>the Third Renaissance</u> - **DIGITAL RENAISSANCE** of the human thought, the time that will take humanity far beyond the terrestrial boundaries in the future. We are merging now with *the Artificial Intelligence* in the most mind-boggling way.

No doubt, <u>robots will be way smarter than us,</u> but I'm sure, the human mind will still be responding better to the *Universal Intelligence of Creation* than future hybrids .The time of the <u>Digital Renaissance</u> must be evolving us in unison with the Creator. The question is **HOW**?

What is the modality of our communication with the Universal Energy Field? How can we establish the unbreakable connection with the **MASTER MIND** that we perceive as God and that is transmitting information to the best of us, able to tune their minds to the divine vibrations. One thing seems to be certain to me - the hybrids won't have any **INTUITION** and **CONSCIOENCE** - our direct lines with the Creator and the basic tools of the Emotional Diplomacy. The problems that we must solve today are not only political, economic, educational; they are holistic, individual, and universal!

Under the pressure of the digital evolution, our personal **DNA** is rapidly changing, making holistic self-development and raising of self-consciousness our goals. **THE SCOPE OF OUR VISION** is changing from narrow, too specified, detail-oriented to a general, strategical, <u>multi-dimensional, multi-disciplinary, and multi-planetary.</u>

To Artificial Intelligence Beware, Let's Be More Holistically Aware!

3. Change the Stylistic Modality of Your Technological Vanity!

Most importantly, we need to urgently focus on developing a new, **holistically educated, self-educated, and technologically educated human being** with a higher level of conscious **SELF-MATURATION** that demonstrates new ethical values and a new stylistic modality of behavior. A technologically prompted modality of our common life on Earth relates to the *"spiritualized intelligence"* that will be perceptive of much higher vibrations of thought and its social, cultural, financial, emotional, psychological, and physical manifestations.

Thoughts and words must not part in the action waltz!

I mean here that our international , racial, and individual problems stem from our general scientific ignorance and the absence of the **ARISTOCRATIC GRAVITY** when we do not mean what we say and you say what you do not mean. We must learn to be responsible for our thoughts, words, emotions, and actions. Only then, can a person call himself / herself a spiritually and technologically mature person. So, **Emotional Diplomacy** is, in fact, the **GRAMMAR OF SELF-MANAGEMENT** and of a self-monitored, Self-Renaissance.

The know-how of such education is our responsibility. Then, we won't get enslaved by the *Super Artificial Intelligence*. We'll monitor it in sync with the Universal Master Mind. We've already become digital extensions of our gadgets, but we must also become conscious, mature, responsible regulators of their future manifestations.

Learn to Fly in the Mind and Be One of the Most Intelligent Kind!

4. A New Reality Based on Mental Gravity!

Under the impact of the universal changes that we are experiencing now, we need to realize our own **MULTI-DIMENSIONAL** nature that is integrating the *physical, emotional, mental, spiritual, and universal realms of life* in us and that is pushing us to conscious realization of what life and successful living are all about. Look around - kids and grown-ups are new technological apps.

We'll be becoming more and more whole and imperfectly perfect, putting the form and the content of our lives in sync by following the **HOLISTIC PARADIGM of SELF-CREATION** and embracing new life parameters. This paradigm indicates if you are moving forward toward your intellectually spiritualized fractal unity, or you are going backward, being a burden to yourself and the people around you. To evolutionary survive, we must put an end to the dissonance between the form + content of our lives, forming solid, holistic **SELF- GRAVITY**.

Form + Content

(Body+ Spirit+ Mind) + (Self-Consciousness + Universal Consciousness)

Living Intelligence + Enlightened Self-Consciousness = Self-Renaissance!

We need to **SELF-REGULATE** living in the digitized world which will hardly be able *to duplicate the fusion of our hearts and minds* for quite some time. That's the exceptional expertise that we need to capitalize on now! Unfortunately, there are very many people on Earth that are **CO-DEPENTDANT** on the society, on a certain person, on fun life. "*Freedom of thought is the most precious freedom in the world.*" *(Albert Einstein)* Your exceptionality is in your innate creativity and a unique personality! Self-Realization is Your Self-Salvation!

(Rule # 8 of Self-Renaissance)

To Be Self-Emancipated; Stop Being Society-Indoctrinated!

5. The Digitized Self-Renaissance

So, to be optimistically inspired by our wonderous **NOW,** we need to monitor our **MULTI-DIMENSIONAL RENAISSANCE** (*physical, emotional ,mental, spiritual, and universal*) in sync with the well-measured and consciously regulated Artificial Intelligence. Using it mindfully, we must first <u>restore our heart + mind broken link</u> that requires a newly conducted *Synthesis – Analysis - Synthesis* insightful research for the biological and technological symbiosis that will help enrich our lives with love. <u>Let's admit, our renaissance is inseparable with it!</u>

The technologically obtained freedom from everyday time-consuming chores should be used for the self-growth and self-renaissance not to let *the Artificial Super-Intelligence* over-power us in every stratum of life. So, we need to maximize our effort on the path of digital extension of ourselves, monitoring the self-growth towards the fractal formation of the <u>form + content</u> link that a machine will never be capable of establishing in sync with the Universal Mind..

Let the simulated reality remain the domain of science and a game!

Self-Renaissance should be performed with the conscious control and <u>the sense of measure</u> so that technology could serve us, not enslave us. I'm sure other more technologically advanced extra-terrestrial civilizations *cannot beat the Creator's evolutionary up-beat*, and most likely haven't done it so far anywhere in the unpredictable *Where?* I see the most positive result of the Artificial Intelligence, Nanotechnology, and Super-Intelligence in the inevitable and most enlightening <u>unification of different branches of science,</u> helping us monitor One common process of every one's **SELF-RENAISSANCE** cognitively, consciously, and technologically. So, let's be spiritually realistic and not overly pessimistic! "<u>The best is yet to come!</u>"

The Digital Extension of You is Your Self-Renaissance, New!

6. Personal Refinement is in the Artificial Intelligence Confinement!

The present-day neuroscience has changed our limited vision of the brain, and it tries to unveil the magic of the mind that surpasses any known machine or any theory about its **complexity.** We know now that *to study means to better the neuron network in the brain*, and every new learning is changing this most artful and intricate network in the world of life. There's a saying in Russian about three most important things in life that determine our happiness in its outcome:

1. Who to be born from.   2. Who to be taught by.   3. And who to marry.

Each concept can be developed into a thesis, but the fundamental one is **who we are taught by** because *the level of our intelligence determines our self-consciousness,* and in the long run, it impacts our entire life. Now, our common life on Earth is enlightened by the Artificial Intelligence. So, let's self – transform to be in the up the par form!.

The world is no longer man-ruled; it's machine-ruled!

True, we are getting more and more entangled into the world of artificial intelligence *physically, emotionally, mentally, spiritually, and universally,* but we must monitor this process holistically, too. Most urgently on this holistic path, we need new **INFORMATION PROCESSING SKILLS** *to master the digital reality authoritatively!*

So, to go with the flow of Self-Renaissance in its each stage, we need to perform **a rigorous selection and organization** of the in-coming information, first. The avalanche of the information that we get every day messes up the mind and confuses the psychological make-up. If going with the flow while driving is a traffic-forced thing, going with the common flow in a private life is a self-worth diminishing thing.

Make Technology Work for Your Self-Ecology!

7. The Sense of Measure Must Be Our Greatest Treasure!

So, *the world is Artificial Intelligence-measured now*, and we need to adjust to it because *"life does not adjust to us, we adjust to life!"* Unfortunately, <u>we lack the sense of measure</u> that we need to monitor our new *physical, emotional, mental, spiritual, and universal realms of life*. The lack of the sense of measure proves that the present-day human being needs to be technologically acculturated, not just educated.

We need the sense of measure most of all in *regulating the avalanche of information* that is overwhelming us now. Unless we learn how to consciously sort out the information and sift it for its validity, coming to the forefront of our evolution and beating the competitive chaos between the biological mind and the artificial one might sweep us off the Self-Renaissance track back onto the road of self-corrode. The machines are way better than us, and *their renaissance might become the end of ours.* Therefore, the digital impact on our human evolution <u>must be measured and regulated consciously.</u> Our social kaleidoscope also needs to be narrowed in color to enable us to single out the people that contribute to our self-growth, not mess it up by luring us with the technological fun-seeking instead of **SELF-SEEKING!**

Life-Gaining is in Self-Taming!

In sum, we are on the path of self-search for either the dead-end or the breakthrough to the impossible, with the mesmerizing outcome – <u>Digital Self-Renaissance.</u> Technology has become a Menacing Luminary of the time , on the one hand, but the most enlightening one, on the other. The Artificial Intelligence is providing *a new degree of self-creative freedom for us,* and we should use it with the benefit for a personal Self-Renaissance in every realm of life..

Technological Regulation + Conscious Self-Formation = Self-Renaissance
Monitored Salvation!

The Sense of Measure is a Great Treasure!

8. Information Processing Skills

Every one of us is an individual, and the information that we are getting in a non-stop way must be individually processed based on <u>new Information-Processing Skills.</u> and the **AWARE ATTENTION** ability that must be developed in kids as early as possible in every of the five circles of life. The time for writing diaries, reading long novels, killing time with a junk book, roaming through pages of the sophisticated and bureaucratically framed information is gone. Let's turn over that page at the information age!

<u>To become One of a kind, let technological order rule your mind!</u>

The speed of the machine-processed information cannot be surmounted by us, but we must work out *the information processing skills* that will help us sift the information for its validity in a new, time-respectful way. <u>The economy of the language must be a Must</u>!

Learn to say what you mean and mean what you say! I'm sure robots are language- sensitive. In information processing and the information receiving, we must also follow the universal life paradigm - *Synthesis – Analysis – Synthesis.* The marketing rules below must match our brain-machines.

Do like me! Do with me! Do better than me!

I keep following this paradigm when structuring the thinking of my students, helping them internalize information, personalize it, and externalize it after they manage to consciously process it through personal *selection and organization* both in their minds and in the machine. Quality and the speed must take a lead!

(Rule # 9 of Self-Renaissance)

Internalize-Personalize- Externalize =

Be Technologically Wise!

9. Technological Inspiration is Our Self-Growth Salvation!

There is no way back to our limited normalcy of the past. The process of **self-reorganization** of our electronically drifted and artificial intelligence enhanced self-consciousness is going on irreversibly. The artificial intelligence is better than us, speed-wise and memory-wise, and before we end up in its totality, we need to be growing in each of us *a new physical, emotional, mental, spiritual, and universal personality*.

Very soon, we'll be taught by our robot friends that will be refining our consciousness. A cast of new generation of people is stepping on the planet Earth. They will be our future bosses, able to merge the simulated reality and the real one! Apparently, we need to develop the **CODEX OF EMOTIONAL DIPLOMACY** for ourselves, humans, and separately, for our communication with the hybrids – the beings with the artificial and human minds fusion. Every one of us needs to update the codex of his own Emotional Diplomacy with the sacred values, based on his / her faith and wisdom.

Take "**Ten Commandment**" as the basis and go from there, being the new reality aware. Unfortunately, we do not study *any codex of behavior* in our schools. Anything connected with the kids' manners and their idea of emotional diplomacy is a tabula rasa. The seeds of emotional intelligence (*Daniel Goleman*) are mostly sowed in us in our families, and that knowledge is never properly rooted in schools and colleges. Emotional intelligence as the basis for the Emotional Diplomacy is the inseparable part of Self-Renaissance. It's a hand to support, an ear to hear someone out, the heart to understand, and the grace to forgive. A new cast of people, our followers, will have *new physical, emotional, mental, spiritual, and universal make-up* that will be totally different. Let's help them be better than us!

Our Holistic Acculturation is in the Emotional Diplomacy Skills Formation!

10. "Don't Teach just the Subject, Teach the Whole Person!" *(Leo Vygotsky)*

As a concerned educator, I've been governed by this statement of my favorite psycholinguist all my professional life. It reminded me to widen the students' general outlook and form their personalities at each lecture. It became the motto of my very successful academic career, and it had never failed me.

The exponential growth of technology requires an <u>exponential growth of intelligence</u> that must be holistically shaped and thus, based on the expanded outlook, not limited by the choice of a major. It must be embracing <u>ten vistas of intelligence</u>, based on the latest scientific developments

<u>Learn to decipher the text of life without any personal strife!</u>

The memory bank of a self-growth-oriented person must be filled up with very well ***sorted out and systematized information*** that is being governed by the **AWARE ATTENTION** of the brain, like a mouse does it on a computer. The attention of a young person should be switched onto new technologically enhanced Self-Creation, not just money-chasing accumulation! **BE SHARP, SHARPER, THE SHARPEST!**

Also, our education needs ***to be student-obsessed***, like business is customer-oriented, meeting their exceptional needs. New knowledge, backed-up technologically and enhanced spiritually needs to re-orient gadget users to self-transformation and self-creation." *The life of service and adventure starts here.***"** *(Reid Hoffman)* We need to focus on the ***holistic education, self-education, and Artificial Intelligence education*** to build up the solid basis for the beyond the terrestrial future. *(See Ten Vistas of Intelligence / Stage Three, mental dimension below)*

The Holistically Based Self-Renaissance is, in fact, the Invention of a New Self-Stance!

11. Holistic Acculturation of Self

In sum, we all need self-awareness, raised self-consciousness, and more consistent work on the **HOLISTIC ACCULTURATION OF SELF.** Such self-acculturation must be a personal business, backed up by the holistic education that should provide us with the **SCIENCE** of **LIFE** and new **INFORMATION-PROCESSING** skills.

Internalize the emotions and externalize the mind. Be One of a kind!

The molecular technology, known as *nanotechnology,* will enhance the power of cognition and the goal of education. I hope that it will monitor the process of the **humanization of technology**, too. Our objective is to stop the de-humanization of our souls. But to accomplish this declared uniqueness, you need to put your **heart and mind in sync**. It's an absolute requirement! Science proves now that a heart has the neurological cells that function as the brain neurons, in total connection with them. The **heart + brain** communication must be at the bottom of our *technological acculturation!*

Our whole life is the process of raising our self-consciousness that is, in fact, **HEART + SPIRIT + MIND** unbreakable connection that is instilled in us by the Universal Consciousness that we call **FAITH.** **The heart + mind sync** is the core demand of the Emotional Diplomacy that is at the bottom of faith. *The ability to harmonize the heart and the mind is the way to become One of a Kind!*

The present-day forking reality of thoughts and emotions suggests we have *a progression in the consonance direction*! This consonance is attainable only if we put ourselves together in our inner and outer lives. Self-Consciousness sorts us out into intelligent and limited, kind and cruel, rough and polite, merciless and compassionate, godly and godless people. **Technology, in contrast, unites us in a conscious fashion!** The process of information processing and its fundamental enrichment with the latest developments in science, or mega-science, changes the scene of today's brutally competitive world. To adjust to it, education needs to be presented as **ONE HOLISTIC SYSTEM** that is prioritizing intelligence as the form and self-consciousness raising as the content of the paradigm: **Internalizing – Personalizing – Externalizing!**

Living Intelligence + Enlightened Self-Consciousness = Self-Renaissance!

Structure is the fundamental principle in everything, not just in science or in a well-run business. We must code ourselves for the best net-outcome, having a clear-cut set of actions in the mind to follow. To put the form and the content of our efforts in sync, be defined by the vision of your future!.

Form + **Content**

(Body+ Spirit+ Mind) + (Self-Consciousness + Universal Consciousness)

Living Intelligence + Enlightened Self-Consciousness = Self-Renaissance!

So, don't follow a common trend; get to the fundamental truth of your own bend!

"It doesn't matter

What others say about me.

Nor does it matter

What they think.

What matters is

What I know about Me,

The rest is empty

Se la vie! " (*Omar Khayyam in my translation*)

The Art of Living is the Art of Digitally Monitored Becoming!

12. I wish I Could Live then, in an Unanswerable When!

In sum, very soon, the codex of our Emotional Diplomacy will be dictated to us by the machine that is already becoming emotionally sensitive and perceptive to our thoughts and feelings We need to start getting prepared for its extra-terrestrial realization *to become beyond the terrestrial people of Steve Jobs , Elon Musk, and Jeff Bezos type.*(See the book "Beyond the Terrestrial"- the universal dimension of life / 2019) I think that to compete with the machines of the future, we will create the information processing machines, working at a much higher level of vibration than the ones that *the computer giants are monitoring us at, now,* monopolizing our social space and threatening to rid us of the motivation to create new technological miracles because they can easily obtain them. But there are no limits for the impossible!

The fear that your creation will immediately be bought and *the authentic possession of the creation* will be absorbed is real We hear predictions like that on TED talks and on You Tube, but I ground my students' doubts and fears and enthuse them to keep creating the impossible, anyway. We cannot see the extraterrestrials yet because we cannot reach their high level of energy vibrations, and that is the problem our present-day young generation will have to solve. *The higher Technological Renaissance will loom, the better Human Renaissance should bloom!*

We need to be in charge, very much! I've been working as a college educator for years, and the *trajectory of the young minds' transformation* has interested me all my life. It has changed from very hungry knowledge-learners, to the information consumers that just need correct channeling. But we can still inspire each mind to be One of a kind! The ingenuity of a human mind is not yet totally defined!

In the Life-Refining Times, We Need Inspired Information Modifiers!

Section 2

You Have to Be Bold to fit in the New Life's Mold!

Our

New Life

Stems

Anything that happens consistently gets linked!

Self-Renaissance is the Faith-Relationship with Yourself!

(Rule # 10 of Self-Renaissance)

Bringing Together our Biological and Digital Realms, We're Constructing Our New Life Stems!

1. *"Art is I; Science is We!"* (*Claude Bernard*)

The exponential growth of technology proves that climbing the scientific heights must be our main self-growth motivational guides! Managing yourself <u>knowingly and consciously</u> is, therefore, changing yourself into a harmonious and noble human being with a solid scientific background and aware attention to life and living. ***But new knowledge shouldn't be commercialized; it must make us wise!***

The process of ***emotional diplomacy creation*** in five levels is essential for our **SPIRITUAL MATURATION** - the universal goal of raising our self-consciousness. I agree with *Dr. Karat Zinn* here who writes, ***"Who we think we are is very small compared to who we really are*<u>!</u>"**

Better be a divine enigma, than a godless stigma!

I connect the path of Self-Renaissance to one of the greatest discoveries of fractals in nature, made by an IBM scientist and professor of mathematics in Yale University, *Benoit B. Mandelbrot.* Following ***Dr. Mandelbrot's discovery***, I think that <u>we are forming our life-fractals,</u> too. Our new, holistic life fractals are now acquiring a new function in the circuitry of digitally spiritualized life energy.

The Fractal Structure of Nature

New Knowledge forms New Human Fractals!

2. Ascending Self-Consciousness Realms

Our life fractals are formed at birth, and they encapsulate our souls that are first developed by our parents. They open our hearts and minds to God by introducing us to the religious paradigm. of their spiritual choice. While we are growing spiritually, it is each one's personal goal **to develop his / her own fractal of spiritual maturation.**

We are responsible to turn our religious make-up into a highly spiritual and personable one on the path of making it universal. That's why I think that the philosophy of **mind + body** that was so brilliantly introduced by *Deepak Chopra*, a famous philosopher of our time, needs to be enriched with a holistic one, as *a holistic paradigm of self-development, mentioned above*. Our new, intellectually spiritualized fractals are:

Body+ Spirit + Mind + Self-Consciousness + Super-Consciousness
(The line of connection with the Universal Mind)

In other words, this paradigm presents the holistic unity of the ***physical, emotional, mental, spiritual, and universal*** levels of our evolutionary development, the levels that self-creation should be based on. Following this holistic paradigm, you will be able to achieve personal self-realization and spiritual self-salvation.

Even though electronic intelligence is ruling the world, it should not rule us. Every one of us needs to retain his / her **uniqueness and exceptionality** and develop themselves into noble and spiritualized human beings with a new vision of the reality, able to create his / her inner perceptive device – the **AUTO-MEDIA** of self-creation that will help establish the unity of the conscious and subconscious minds to make us more spiritually mature.

Thus, we'll be Developing New Life Fractals of Holistically Developed Beings.

3. Our New, Holistic "We-Renaissance"!

The new life fractals that we are forming now with the help of technology are being based on digitally-expanded intelligence that shapes **a new holistic self-concept**, *(See " My Ode to Life' above)* the concept of the people that are blazing the trail of the computer science and are changing the world in an evolutionary way. **"*Our seeing requires a correction of mind; just as clear vision requires a correction of the eyes. "*(Alan W. Watts)** Changing ourselves and contributing our best to the world, we generate a new concept of the holistic **"WE - RENAISSANCE,"**, as the concept of the global social unification and mutual responsibility for the life on Earth. ***Our digitally generated connectedness*** forms the society's and the world's consciousness..

The Grid of Consciousness Integration

Super Level	*Consciousness of God!*	*Universal Dimension*
Macro Level	*Consciousness of the Universe*	**Spiritual Dimension**
Mezzo Level	*Consciousness of the World*	**Mental Dimension**
Meta level	*Consciousness of the Society*	**Emotional Dimension**
Micro Level	*Consciousness of a Man*	**Physical Dimension**

The **We-Concept**, or consciousness of the society and the world, presented above is being formed by an unprecedented socialization and globalization of our lives and minds and our gradual self-consciousness ascending. We are, in fact developing ***the holistic consciousness of inter-dependency***. The new **We-Concept** is also emerging in us as the result of our growing digital integrity and ingenuity.. Your head antenna must be set up to receive the messages that you actualize in life, when your self-consciousness in on.

(Rule # 11 of Self-Renaissance)

"As it is Above, so, it is Below!"

4.Don't Be Slow! Reinvent Yourself on the Go!

A dynamic interplay of human consciousness that is changing rapidly with the technological evolution, demands every one's **re-invention of Self,** or **SELF-CONQUERING** in five levels: *physical, emotional, mental, spiritual, and universal holistically.* The five books (See Book Rationale) on **personality geology** call on us to *put our minds and hearts in synch to obtain the fractal symmetry of life* that, according to *Dr. Steven Weinberg,* the Noble Prize winner, *"is underlying everything."* So, the main rule of Self-Renaissance becomes:

Intellectualize your heart and emotionalize the mind!

Be One of a kind!

More particularly, the holistic philosophy of self-development that I am outlining here is meant to back you up in your self-installation by way of enhancing the growth of self-consciousness in a beautiful symmetry with the Universal mind. The individualized vision of life comes with full awareness of what life is all about at its digital upheaval now. If you are not moving forward, you'll be swept off the surface of life as a useless element on the path of exponential evolution.

We need to move the best qualities, instilled in us initially by the **Ten Commandments** to the forefront of our minds to be able to use them to our mutual advantage, de facto, not just de juror. We must **synthesize** *the form and the content of the inner and outer lie* in accord with the present moment first to get more aware of life in general. Next, we need **to analyze** the life we live by becoming more rational and consciousness- driven. Finally, we will establish connection with to the Universal Intelligence, make individualized conscious decisions and accomplish the right outcome in life, getting to the final **synthesis** of our well-lived lives.

Self-Synthesis – Self- Analysis – Self-Synthesis!

5. Our Human Essence is in Self-Renaissance

The fractal vision of life comes with full awareness. To be able to apply the holistic paradigm, presented above to life, you need to have more awareness of life and "live in the Now"*(Eckhart Tolle)* with the goal of raising self-consciousness consciously and holistically. Awareness means to be aware of life" *as is"* without any judgement, with full acceptance of the gift of life. Freeing the spirit and raising self-consciousness is everyone's individual responsibility now. Developing ourselves, we need to live in the mind + heart indivisible unity that turns on our inner barometer - conscience + intuition. So, make your heart smart and the mind kind. Be one of a kind!

Unfortunately, the future of our human souls does not seem to be very promising in view of the accelerating development of cold, inhuman intelligence that yet lacks spiritual insightfulness. Due to high tech explosion, life has a different narrative of self-erosion that we need to re-direct to the holistic unity of our fractal formation with the new technology in sync as our main friend, not foe on the evolutionary go.

Body + Spirit + Mind+ Self-Consciousness + Super-Consciousness

There is also another reason for which self-development is extremely timely and should be paid extra attention to. The time of an unprecedented socialization of our lives *pollutes us in the core and demands ecological attempts* on our part to be doubled in soul-refining effort. There is order and harmony in the Universal Intellect that we are part of, but we are disturbing it with our "***collective unconscious.***" *(Carl Yung)* The time for unconscious, confrontational living has expired. We need to consciously regulate and monitor our personal evolution.

"The Entire Universe is a System of Fractals." *(David Wilcock)*

6. Inner Symmetry and Personal Gravity

In five books on **Self-Resurrection**, level by level, I remind you about the parallel between the **fractal geometry in nature** and the fractal formation of our inner symmetry or **PERSONAL GRAVITY.**

A human being is an almost perfect creation, with the golden section of proportion, balance, and beauty of its own, and each of us has his / her own "**golden ration**" with the infinite number of qualities, streaming to perfection. So, the statement "*No one is perfect*" is not justifiable. A self-renaissance oriented person is forming a fractal of a self-realized, self-fulfilling being with a **NEW LIFE STEM** of inner symmetry.

Body+ Spirit + Mind + Self-Consciousness + Super-Consciousness

Staying on this path of **the intuitive self-discovery**, you become aware of your exceptional mission on Earth, and what's most important, you discover this mission yourself. You will start forming your life's **FRACTAL UNITY**, following the example of the most advanced people that have accumulated **SELF-GRAVITY**, based on self-awareness, **the sense of self-worthiness**, and the Emotional Diplomacy Skills, *changing their physical, emotional, mental, spiritual, and universal rituals* of life and forming new pattens of behavior.

Self-transformation is an inner symmetry formation!

So, we need to holistically develop this unity in five levels corresponding to five stages of a **NEW LIFE STEM** – Self-Awareness, Self-Monitoring, Self-Installation, Self-Realization, and Self-Salvation.

These stages must be developed *in the integral unity* in which the mini-self-universe is absorbed by the Super Universe of life, making your life shine with a new holistic meaning!

Everything We Do Must Be Strategized into a System, too!

7. Form + Content of Life = Self-Renaissance

In sum, we often hear the question, *"What's he / she worth?"* and the answer to this question has a common monetary evaluation. But our souls are not valued by our bank accounts. They are the reflection of the integral unity of the five main aspects of self-growth. We are monitored by the evolutionary paradigm of the life - death - life cycle that incorporates five stages of a person's self-growth. *(physical, emotional ,mental, spiritual, universal)., channeled by the universal paradigm of life formation.*

Self-Synthesis ⟹ **Self-Analysis** ⟹ **Self-Synthesis!**

(Self-Awareness) → *(Self-Monitoring + Self-Installation +Self-Realization* → *(Self-Salvation)*

Together, the stages of self-growth constitute **the form + content** of our lives in an unbreakable connection. If we are consciously sustaining this unity in us, we'll become more enthused with life in its ups and downs. **AUTHENTICITY AND SINCERITY** will be instilled back into our emotional gravity! Meanwhile, our homes are the sandcastles and our loved ones suffer due to our lack of responsibility. Such situations are generated by the lack of *Emotional Diplomacy Skills* and a weak willpower for their conscious implication that results in our present-day the heart-mind disconnection.

An impersonal attitude is like a regular fake gratitude.

A raised self-consciousness means a better family life, better children, a better society! Intelligence, nobility, kindness, and faith must become the **SELF GRAVITY CORE** of a new age **ARISTOCRATIC PERSONALITY** without a materialistic vanity. *"Only by the act of triggering the neurons of the heart and the brain, we'll become better people."* (Gregg Brandon)

Living Intelligence + Enlightened Self-Consciousness = Personal Gravity!

8. Stability of the Internal World

In sum, at the time of the technological turmoil, I see the stability of the internal world in the **Synthesis -Analysis – Synthesis** fort. It helps us see ourselves as <u>Self-Resurrected people</u>, *able to co-feel and co-create, not just survive , compete, and self-obliterate.*

The electro-magnetic field, generated by the <u>heart+ mind unity</u> is channeling us toward the unification of our hearts and minds in a family, at work, in the society at large. The holistic formula of life, presented here as <u>the fractal of our spiritual maturation,</u> can be applied to our conscious information processing.

(Body+ Spirit + Mind) + (Self-Consciousness + Super-Consciousness)

<u>(Synthesis -Analysis – Synthesis</u> **or** <u>Internalize - Personalize – Externalize)</u>

(Internalizing the knowledge of life - Personalizing it in the process of self-creation, and Externalizing it, completing the assigned from the Above mission)

This holistic formula of life should be studied, reasoned out, and become the second nature with every human being on Earth. Each life must be *self-individualized* and cultivated by a person *physically, emotionally, mentally, spiritually, and universally*, and the know-how of such general education or **SELF-EDUCATION** must be provided. (*See the Introduction*). That's what the main incentive of all my books is.

Technological miracles of the Super Artificial Intelligence will eventually <u>create a robot that might have self-awareness</u> , his own *"I AM."* identity. It'll be a truly dangerous time for the human civilization because that *machine-generated awareness* will create its own plans in life, its own motives for action, and we might literally be in the way of those plans, but. <u>it should not become a dead-end for our souls.</u> No machine will ever be able to experience the sincere human depth and a *conscious awareness of the ability to love and to be loved in return.*

"No Seed Grows Without Support." (*Proverbs 19, 6*)

Life's Path from Birth is Heaven on Earth!

(Best Photos - Internet Collection)

Charge Your Self-Renaissance Flight with a Lot of Spiritual Might!

Section 3

Be a Sage on Your Personal Stage!

Life-Essence
is in a Conscious
Self-Renaissance!

Use the present-day technology to maintain your

Self-Monitored Inner Ecology!

(Rule # 12 of Self-Renaissance)

Adjust to the New Reality Without Any Ignorant Vanity!

1. Our New, Holistic Culture of Being!

Generalizing the above presented ideas, the goal of your work on self-renaissance is to instill in Self the **HOLISTIC LIFE MANAGEMENT SKILLS**, based on the technological acculturation that is the essence of our survival in the new **Super Artificial Intelligence re-focused reality.** But the Master Mind is still ruling it ,*and we should never destroy that line of connection that we yet need to decipher.* We have a new type of communication now **MAN + MACHINE SYMBIOSIS** - *a universal oasis of thought and matter,* and each of us is part of it too, only if we consciously monitor it.

Like the refraction of sunlight makes the sky seem blue by day and orange by sunset, the information that we are getting now *gets refracted in every mind and heart* and makes us act in a new way. Therefore, you need **to consciously monitor this process**, learning to process information differently, sifting it from messy redundancy and leaving only the stuff that your **AWARE ATTENTION** singles out.

We need to choreograph our aware attention in the infinite body of information, stored in the digital memory of the Universe. I do the same here, presenting only easily digestible, technologically friendly, page-long chunks of information for your consideration. Also, try to *retain the objectivity of your vision.* Like the bending of the light waves, the life information ,singled out by your aware attention gets infracted through the prism of your *Holistic Being* in five stages of life - **micro** (*physical level*) - **Life Awareness**; **meta** (*emotional level*) - **Self-Monitoring**; **mezzo** (*mental level*) - **Self-Installation**; **macro** (*spiritual level*) – **Self-Realization**; and **super** (*universal level*)– **Self-Salvation.** Stay in the flow of the technologically monitored self-reformation go.

(Rule # 13 of Self-Renaissance)

Being the Best is a Tough Test!

2. Carry Light; Light is Our Might!

Next, **perceive the necessity to carry light inside for the people as a mission.** Change the inner paradigm of the society-indoctrinated dogmas of expecting someone to make you happy, rushing into quick-fix relationships, changing jobs, leaving the loved ones and betraying kids. Stop seeking places where grass is greener, and life is more lucrative and pleasurable **Be the doers of your reality; not its product!**

When self-development is at bay, degradation is at play!

Inner unity is obtained by means of friction – **the inner struggle between YES and NO** in your life circle - **body + spirit+ mind+ self-consciousness + super-consciousness!** In this struggle, do not forget that the free choice that you have is the choice to either go with the common flow and be constantly entangled in different compromises against our own Self or to swim against the current and feel free to do what your intuition and unique **EXCEPTIONALITY** prompt to you.

It is the choice to create yourself into a beautiful human being that other people enjoy being around. So, the process of **Self-Renaissance** is about managing life and yourself **knowingly, consciously, and respectfully!** Gradually but surely, you will be getting free of our old habits and detachments, old memories and dirty fun impulsivity. Also, to become an integral part of the new reality, you need to restore love in your heart and sincerity in our mind. There is too much fakeness inside and outside of us, and many people lose their spiritual gravitation and fall into degradation! It's crucial to let the digitally enhanced space in your mind be enlightened with new Self-Awareness. Every day becomes the proof of the validity of your initial creation status that reminds you to consciously monitor the fractal Self.

(Rule # 14 of Self-Renaissance)

In My Life Quest, I'm the Best!

3. The Greatest Art of All is to Emotionally Self-Install!

Technologically enhanced living demands a conscious culture of the emotional being! There cannot be any talk about self-renaissance unless you study your **psychological / emotional keyboard** and learn to quickly recognize and re-program your negative emotions. Self-Awareness will also help you do it tactfully with the loved ones and other people. It takes only a stroke to change a minus into a plus and take charge of the consequences, thus. **Make your heart smart and the mind kind! Be One of a kind!** The way you monitor your heart + mind link is who you are today and who you'll be tomorrow.

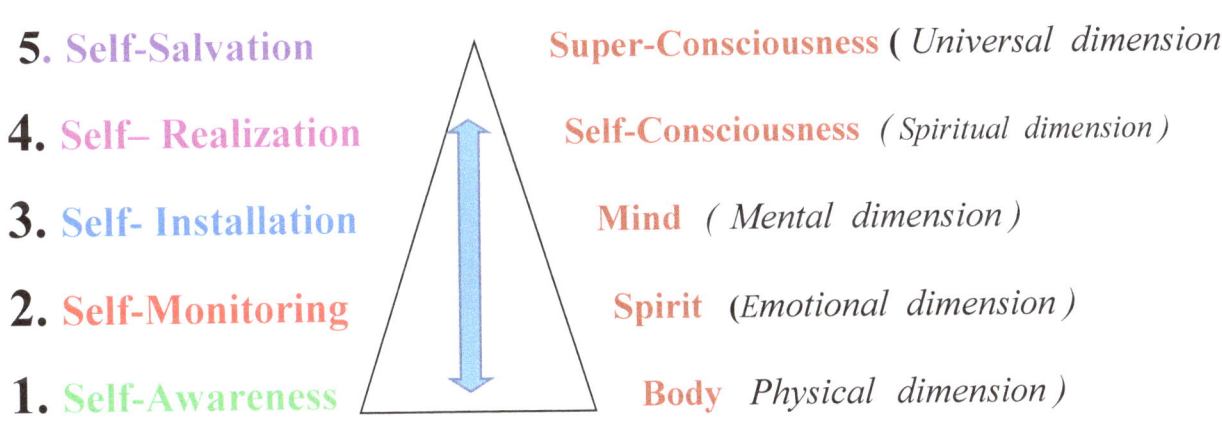

5. Self-Salvation	**Super-Consciousness** (*Universal dimension*
4. Self– Realization	**Self-Consciousness** (*Spiritual dimension*)
3. Self- Installation	**Mind** (*Mental dimension*)
2. Self-Monitoring	**Spirit** (*Emotional dimension*)
1. Self-Awareness	**Body** *Physical dimension*)

" **Aware vision is an all-inclusive process**. " (*Sadhguru*)

Visualize this holistic system to monitor your self-growth consciously, placing the focus of your **AWARE ATTENTION** on *the Emotional Diplomacy Skills* in the inseparable unity with the entire paradigm of **Self-Renaissance.** *Active and Passive meditations* (*See" Methodology of Self-Ecology" below*) will help you mobilize yourself for holistic **SELF-ACTUALIZATION,** without any **IMPULSIVITY** and frustration.

Make Your Life Processed through the Self-Monitored Happiness!

4. To Feel Complete, Be New Spiritual Knowledge and Information Upbeat!

Also, new times generate new knowledge and new interpretation of the old religious dogmas. Religion has contributed a lot to our spiritual growth, and the sacred books must remain our initial source of knowledge, faith and wisdom.. But many dogmatic standpoints that have worked for twenty centuries have **changed their conceptual meaning** at the time of our technologically enhanced breakthroughs. Two thousand years later, we are beginning to realize that **Christ's philosophy of love and self-growth** of discovering the Heaven within is what we desperately need. now. But it must be reasoned out by us on the path of the technologically enhanced Self-Renaissance.

Body + Spirit + Mind) + (Self-Consciousness + Universal Consciousness = A Whole You!

At the heart of every world religion is the concept of *the Absolute, the Unknowable, the Infinite, and the Source*, as well as the moral standards and the messages that are essentially the same and that the best of us follow, irrespective of different spiritual leaders in the mind. True, the new reality is too stressful, speed-accelerated, information over-loaded, and too complex, but it's our world now.

We have become too simple and media-primitivized for this world. So, install a new *physical, emotional, mental, spiritual, and universal* landscape into your minds and **work on grounding** the bothering you habits, attachments, weaknesses with consciously monitored breathing. **Breathe in health - breath out sickness**. Breathe in love- breathe out indifference, etc. Breathing out any negative emotion consciously, you must visualize it being grounded deeply into the Earth for reformation. Unload your beautiful soul for a better-monitored self-control!

The Holistic Education is in Establishing
Emotional Gravity and Mental Sanity!

5. Time is Right to Accumulate New Technologically Enhanced Personal Might!

In our hard-wired present-day life, we all need to develop the ability _to regulate our emotional pendulum,_ not to let it swing too much *to the left* (*the negative swing*), loaded with hate, racism, envy, and depression, or too much *to the right* (*the positive swing*), enhanced with too much fun-seeking and hyper emotions addicting.

Emotional Gravity is an educational thing!

So, try with the help of this book to instill   in yourself *the basic Emotional Diplomacy Skills* and break your stale emotional habits that are stored in the subconscious mind and do not let you re-wind a much more creative and productive mind. _The emotional intelligence_ (*see a great book by Daniel Goleman)* must be an essential subject at school to help kids *get the basics of Emotional Diplomacy as early as possible*. I integrate my ideas about Emotional Diplomacy here with the inspirational auto-suggestive background because a dry theory bores and has a reverse effect on the mind.

Mind + Heart integration is the base for a happy life's elation!.

Very soon, we'll have robot friends that will help us control our emotions, and I'm sure they will sound better if their timely advice will rhyme in the form of *the psychologically backed up, inspirational mind-sets*. It's easier to remember the rhyming lines that _resonate in the heart and the mind_ and help you consciously stabilize yourself. You can upload them to your smart phone and have them at hand when there is no second wind in your inner twit.

(Rule # 15 of Self-Renaissance)

Use Advanced Technology for Your Emotional Self-Ecology!

6. Personal Gravity Forms a Personality!

The skill of <u>selection and organization</u> (_Section 1_) of the in-coming information must be developed in our present-day technologically messed up minds. **The mind must be working in synch with its two main brains** - the conscious and the sub-conscious ones.

The unity of both brains is the sign of a holistically developed **PERSONAL GRAVITY** that the real doers of life , such as _Steve Jobs, Elon Musk, Bill Gates, Reid Hoffman, Jeff Bezos_ and many other advanced businessmen and scientists have. They are pushing our evolutionary development beyond the terrestrial boundaries against any odds Their life path is full of obstacles and personal strife, but they self-manage them with their personal might! Their self-renaissance is on the service for the humanity! **They are beyond the terrestrial people!**

So, go forth and become your PERSONAL GRAVITY boss!

People with mental-emotional gravity have a rare ability to predict how things would play out in the future. Only such minds are oriented toward the spontaneity of creative thinking that is again <u>the heart + mind infusion.</u> It is an extraordinary ability, that _only aware attention-focused people_ have, able to cut the Gordian knots in any problematic situation and get on with accomplishing their unique goal.

According to _Dr. Bruce Lipton_ such qualities can be developed because we are not predisposed by our hereditary DNA to be brainy or brainless, to be second-rate people or geniuses. We can develop such qualities if we change our perception of life from unconscious and pre-programmed to <u>the fully conscious and self-reprogrammed</u>. Such skills, however, must be self-developed.

Only with the Mind's Clarity, Emotional Normalcy, and Absence of Polarity Can <u>We Generate Personal Gravity!</u>

7. Aristocracy of Emotional Diplomacy!

In the description of the Aristocratic Trajectory for Self-Renaissance I have provided above the two pyramids, presenting *"The Best of Me!" and " The Worst of Me "* images in five   strata for an objective **SELF-SCANNING**. Below, you can read a description of Self that might help you systematize the Ultimate Result Vision of Self on the path of *personal gravity accumulation.*

I'm not static; I'm holistically aristocratic!

To begin with, in the physical realm of my life, I can complement myself on having good health habits, being industrious, reliable, responsible, honest, and demonstrating a high self-worth and self-esteem.

In the emotional stratum, I'm reserved, agreeable, communicative, friendly, helpful and able to display the ability to tame my tongue anger, impulsivity, and the sex drive. I'm self-confident and constructive on the path of realizing my unique exceptionality.

In my mental dimension, I am interesting to others because I get interested in life and its progress.. I'm knowledgeable and very professional .I'm creative and able to strategize my thoughts , bringing them to a needed result. I'm an assertive leader, demonstrating financial intelligence and determination. I can accomplish the impossible, led by the mind-set **I can! I want to…! And I will!**

On the spiritual vector of life, I'm full of faith and spiritualized intelligence. *My heart and mind are in sync,* and I'm conscious and intuitive, kind and forgiving in my dedication to evil fighting in myself and around me.

In the Universal dimension of my life, I can admit that I am firm in the decision *to raise my consciousness* and *realize my exceptionality* as my appreciation of the gift of life , granted to me.

According to the holistic paradigm, your self-image is supposed to go through *the stages* of generalization, selection, and strategizing in your personality growth. Mind you, the stages of self-creation that are presented as the matrix of the self-gravity accumulation and the holistic paradigm of self-consciousness formation are structured by the systemic formula:

Self-Synthesis ⟹ *Self-Analysis* ⟹ *Self-Synthesis!*

8. Mind is Logical, but Life is Not!

In the Introduction to the book, I indicate that the purpose of this book is **informational, re-formational, and inspirational**, I try to create an ***objective and time-sustainable blueprint of self-creation*** (*chunk 3 above*), that can be refilled with new knowledge but remain structurally the same. There is no system without the structure! It is an overview of self-discovery, presented in page-long, digestible and technologically friendly **plan of action**, that can work for everyone in its structurally holistic **"SIMPLEXITY."**

Admittedly, we do not know how 100 billion neurons of the brain get into a system. The speed of the neurons in our brains is much lower than that of a computer. The mind, however, is still much more perceptive than a computer. The answer is in the richness of our inner world that is connected to the Universal Intelligence by the **AUTO-ANTENNA** through which we must constantly ***"tune up to the station "God,"*** unifying our different religiously modified perceptions into One.

As per science**, *the Universal Consciousness is digital.*** So, only the conscious mind's fluctuations can win the competition with ignorance that *"still remains the main enemy of the humanity."* (*Albert Einstein*)So, intellectual growth must be inseparable with our emotional maturation that charges our thoughts. In my paradigm of ***Self-Resurrection,*** I provide the holistic blueprint of **SELF-CULTURE,** enriching it with **auto-suggestive, inspirational, and rhyming mind-sets,** that are re-programming the mind to retain the orderly structure of self-creation for years to come. Have this structure in your mind and ***channel it to its fractal unity*** that I managed to install in the minds of my students.

Self-Awareness - Self-Monitoring - Self-Installation - Self-Realization – Self-Salvation!

"Simplexity" = Simplicity + Complexity!

9. Become a Much Wiser Life-Actualizer!

In sum, our parents initially create and shape our personal world. First, we get the inherited traits of character, then the ones, formed by them, and the rest of our lives, *we are shaping our own personalities ourselves* under the effect of the environment. We live our lives with either no regrets, or we waste our lives.

Life ends either with vexation or full self-realization.

The Law of Sow and Reap is directly connected to the *life-loving auto-suggestive work* that is outlined below. But first, create a vision of Self ten or twenty years from now. Be stubborn in your vision! Evolved thoughts always give a boost to constructive, reasoned out actions that are governed in us by the *Universal Intelligence* that we perceive as God. We mindfully set-up the *auto-media* divine contact during meditation, praying, or auto-suggestive self-coding. Don't daydream blindly! Be immune to unconscious, automatic living and mind-brewing!

The purity of your intention should be of the highest dimension!

Every chunk of information in this book starts and ends with a self-induction of *an inspirational, will-power sowing character.* I am sure that you have noted by now that almost every paragraph on these pages is concluded with *the mind-sets of an inductive character.* Such auto-suggestibility is meant to boost your spirit and strengthen the determination to stay on the **SELF-INSTALLATION** path that is tricky now. It will accentuate the *value of your life and its mesmerizing beauty,* channeled by the plan of action that I call the Inspirational Psychology for Self-Ecology.

(Rule # 16 of Self-Renaissance)

Life-Gaining is in Self-Training!

9. So, Envision the Scenario of Being
Your Self-Renaissance Empresario!

There is no Self-Worth
Re-defining without the
Emotional Diplomacy
Refining!

Self-Synthesis ⟶ *Self-Analysis* ⟶ *Self-Synthesis!*

(Self-Awareness) → *(Self-Monitoring + Self-Installation +Self-Realization)* → *(Self-Salvation)*

It's Not just the Question of
Manners and Morality. It's the
Question of Living Sensibly
without Materialistic Vanity!

(Rule # 17 of Self-Renaissance)

Don't Be Soul-Bare; Be Soul-Aware!

Part Two of the Book

(Synthesis - Analysis - Synthesis structure of the book)

Auto-Suggestive Psychology

for Self-Ecology!

(Analysis)

Self-Coding is Soul-Rewarding!

(Rule # 18 of Self-Renaissance)

Strengthen Your Personal Gene with the Self-Suggestive Hygiene!

Assume the Burden of Controlling Your Thoughts and Words!

(Best Photos -The internet Collection)

Being Godly is a Godless World is a Challenge and a Reward!

Section 1

Create a New, Mind-Based Vintage You!

The KNOW-HOW
of the
Self-Renaissance
WOW!

(The Self Engaging Technique of the Mind + Heart Link!)

The Self-Resurrective Power of NOW is in your

Consciously Monitored Technological WOW!

(Rule # 19 of Self-Renaissance)

Intuition is the Code of the Heart + Mind Intuitive Suggestion!

1. Help Comes from the Above!

"Emotional Diplomacy" was my first inspirational book, very primitive in the series of 17 other books, written in five dimensions - physical, emotional, mental, spiritual, and universal.

But the idea to write inspirational, psychologically backed-up auto-suggestive boosters and later books on Holistic Self-Creation started with that first book, prompted to me in the most unusual way, literally, from the Above This revelation hit me after **Sep. 11, 2001** events when my daughter, a recent college graduate, who was in the Trade Center on that terrible day, miraculously survived.

Since neither of us had a medical insurance then, getting her back to life appeared to be the challenge that destroyed both of us. Then, one day, I experienced a very weird de-ja-vu. On the way to the college, my mind started creating inspirational boosters in an assay form *(Introduction, Body, Conclusion.)*

The ideas were psychologically based, rhyming and seemed to be dictated to me from the Above. I stopped the car and jotted the first one down. Never in my life had I composed any rhyming lines, being mostly focused on serious academic topics. I decided to take advantage of such revelation to help my daughter see the light at the end of the tunnel and get her out of a fearful oblivion in which she kept muttering, full of agony," *Mom, planes, planes…"*

Being a doctor of Psycholinguistics, I realized then that I got the sign to integrate Psychology and the language in an inspirational way that could help my daughter heal her totally broken spirit herself, using the auto-suggestive programming, or the rhyming **MIND + SPIRIT** boosting. *The result was amazing!* My inspirational boosters and mind-sets brought Yolanta back to reality in which she later wrote four inspirational books for kids, one being *"Fly Like Icarus!"*

Self-Coding is Mind-Rewarding!

2. Good Mood is Our Psychological Food!

I became even more motivated with the inspirational venue of my self-expression after I read about the phenomenon of **Norman Kachsince,** the man who defeated death with smiles and laughter, proving to us that if a person is depressed, his immune system is down because ***the microphages*** (*the blood bodies that are responsible for the purity of blood*) are sleeping. Once a person starts smiling and consciously perceiving the reality, the microphages wake up immediately and start cleansing the blood of the impurities with enthusiasm.

Our thought-forms must be in the Emotional Diplomacy uniforms!

Also, the breakthroughs in digital biology (*Dr. Bruce Lipton*) prove that we can no longer live by the formula , *"It's my DNA. I can't do anything about it!"* It's an outdated view that is disconnected with *the Universal Intelligence* that we must stay in sync with according to our new, digitally enhanced vision of the world - the connection between the **Body Consciousness** and **the Consciousness Body of the Universe.**

It means that the state of our self-consciousness is affected by the mind that, in turn, affects the state of consciousness in our cells. *Dr. Bruce Lipton* calls on us ***"to program our mind-body consciousness at the cellular level"*** that is vibrationally directly connected to the Universal Consciousness, enveloping us everywhere.

So, every booster in this book is **a conceptual, psychologically charged mind-set with a certain message**, sometimes provocative, yet meaningful and well-wishing. Interestingly, these inspirational boosters are not made up by me in the throes of poetic creativity. They just come to me like that, unchanged, once a psychological concept hits the mind..

" Those Who Have Ears, Hear."

3. Biological and Digital Realms are Constructing *New Life Stems!*

I keep testing the *Holistic Paradigm of Self-Creation* with my students who always become very inspired and their uniqueness-refined, having visualized *this plan of action of Self- Creation* in their minds. They up-load the inspirational auto-suggestive mind-sets that resonate with them into their smart phones, boosting their spirit and refreshing the mind. **Technologically monitored cells CAN change your negative Self!**

The changes are also happening in the psyche and the emotional make - up of the young people who inspired me to write the books on *Self-Resurrection.*

I'm more than happy to watch them use the rhyming, psychologically based and easily memorized mind-sets as **SELF-BOOSTERS** in life. Their need for simple, technologically friendly, and scientifically verified **KNOW-HOW** for self-creation goes far beyond their professional intelligence plans. As *Jeff Bezos* says, *"Choose the passion. Don't wait for a passion or a career to choose you!"* **Make your self-worth your main boss!**

Young people want full self-realization and **the recognition of their exceptionality** that I help them discover in themselves. I encourage them to just *choose any book* that helps identify the level of failure in their self-growth (*physical, emotional, mental, spiritual, universal*) and pick the answers to the questions that might be bothering them.

That's the Bible-like psychological **SELF-HELP** at hand at the time of a desperately needed **support for self-management**. There is no need to read the books consequentially. Also, any chunk of information in them may be easily updated online

Order Generates Knowledge and Charges Us with *Personal Magnetism!*

4. Inspirational Methodology of Self-Ecology!

We are all part of One Human Soul that doesn't discriminate us by color, nationality, religion, or the material status. We love, suffer, express happiness or frustration in the same region of the brain - *Amygdala.* **If we clarify the emotions, you'll clarify the mind!** So, let's re-boot the emotional memory shoot! We need to do it auto-suggestively re-programming ourselves .Life is not a rehearsal; it's your reflection in it as a person that needs inspiration continuously.

To get inspired, be self-inspiring!

In order to tame the chaos around you and inside you, you need to auto-suggestively establish the connection between ***the brain and the mind,*** *the heart and the mind,* ***the spirit and the emotions*** that are stored in the subconscious mind as your habits. Habits are much more difficult to re-program than to develop new skills. Habits condition our impulsive behavior, disregarding the superiority of the mind. Only with a clear-cut plan of action, applied consciously, can such self-transformation be achievable. "*The body is a conditioned mind..*"(*Dr. Joe Dispenza*).**Language is the means of coding the mind,** and it needs to be consciously used in the rhyming, authoritative way that constitutes the short-cut to the brain. Your mind is the boss, language is its servant.

" **Language is also the means of fighting death!** (*Dr.Chernigovskaya)*

So, you need to inspire the mind auto-suggestively, using the inspirational mind-sets that get easily memorized or that you find quickly in the smart phone, in the file ***Self-Resurrection.*** In other words, you must work with the mind **authoritatively and inspirationally**. It's our best friend! The focus must be put on the ***brain-mind*** and ***mind-brain*** relationship, monitored consciously by you..

Mind-Refining is Life-Redefining!

5. The Gravity of Self-Worth is Your Force!

How we think and what we feel must be in your conscious control! Thus, you'll create the state of being in which deciphering of the text of life correctly starts with **forcefully deleting from the memory your past mistakes**, frustrations, and self-guilt to demonstrate a new, consciously monitored **EMOTIONAL CULTURE** to ourselves and others.

"A familiar past becomes the predictable future."(Dr .Joe Dispenza) Dr. *Dispenza* explains to us how our conditioned thinking creates the same behaviors. Turns out, *"we hardwire the brain in the same circuits."* This operational and insightful knowledge forms better Self-Awareness that stabilizes us and creates the **GRAVITY OF SELF-WORTH.** (See the book "Self- Worth", 2020)

Another indispensable practice for everyone is meditation. Meditation is about getting still and focused, inwardly disciplined and self-regulated. I like *Dr.Dispenza's* method of meditation, the Transcendental Meditation (*Dr. John Hagelin)*, and the Inner Engineering (*Sadhguru*) a lot.

Meditation is the Code against Self-Erode!

My Auto-Suggestive Meditation, described below is less sophisticated, but very affective too, as an active, supplementary one. *Mastering any meditation is the purpose of synchronizing our being with the Universe* at least at the dilettante level. In the active *Auto-Suggestive Meditation,* the most actionable thing, though, is to have the blueprint of self-growth in the mind all the time.

Our neuroscience has great breakthroughs in this direction. Therefore, *it's vital for our education to provide the basic knowledge about the brain* because without it, students cannot obtain true professional, time needed intelligence.

Hamper the Uncontrolled Way that Leads to Emotional Dismay!

6. Mind-Monitored Self-Taming

In sum, with the *Auto-Suggestive dictum*, you will feel the power of **self-taming and self-refining.** You will feel good, more goal-oriented and, more accomplished in all *five cycles of life- physical, emotional, mental spiritual, and universal.* Order generates self-content and restores the inner balance.

The Active Auto-Suggestive Meditation will provide you with the mind-sets you need in a stressful situation. You can find the one that you need in the file *"Self-Resurrection "*of your smart phone. That's why I recommend that my students organize the information in their smart phones that are becoming more and more the extension of their minds Other than that, active meditation will *restore a good feeling about yourself* that is an indication that you are on the right track of your well-lived day, week, month, year, life. The mind-set below, gets a whole new, personally justifiable meaning.

In My Life Quest, I'm the Best!

Passive Meditation, referred to as" *the bliss body state"* *(Sadhguru)*-harmonizes all the processes in the body and helps us get in touch with the Creator. It's an indispensable part of our life now, essential for out health and the immune system In **Active Meditation**, you do not delve into yourself, *you wake yourself up to conscious, positive action!* A great American scientist and innovator *George van Tassel* , working on the means of life-extension, discovered that *"we may get information through our mental states"* even without a direct contact with the Divine. **Every one of us has a hidden coded program** that we may activate either with the help of *electrical impulses* that revitalize the cells in the body, or we may affect them positively via our own mental connections if we activate them knowingly and consciously. Wow!

Active Meditation Generates Inner Elation!

The Mind-Monitored Bend is the Grammar of Self-Manage-ment!

. Your life depends on the way you operate your mind, language-wise.

(Rule # 20 of Self-Renaissance)

Level by Level, Enforce Your Self-Gravity with Physical, Emotional, Mental, Spiritual, and Universal Sanity!

Self-Management is in the Precision with the Highest Dimension Vision!

(Best Photos - Internet Collection)

Enlighten Your Path with Balance, Belief, and the Light Mass!

1. Inner Harmony is the Soul's Symphony!

We literally need *"to break the habit of being Self"* (*Dr. Rispenza*) and create a new, **Mind-Based Vintage Being!** It's not an easy thing to be done, but it's not altogether impossible if you have the plan of action in the mind and follow it consistently and consciously.

Body + Spirit + Mind) + (Self-Consciousness + Universal Consciousness = A Whole You!

Change requires **synchronizing all these parts of your inner Self** with the help of Emotional Diplomacy Skills that are supposed to instill in you the ability to operate our own emotional keyboard better and not to destroy the emotional keys of others. I suggest following a very simple **Auto-Suggestive Methodology of Self-Ecology** that invites you to re-program the mind and the emotions with the help of my *holistic paradigm of Self-Resurrection (See above)* backed up with the inspirational boosters and mind-sets. (*www.language-fitness. com. Video - in the section Self-Resurrection*)

Self-perfection is a never-ending job of life that needs to be constantly enhanced with **SELF-INDUCTING** or **SELF-PROGRAMMING**. It means that you declare your uniqueness to yourself and the world every day and everywhere, proving it with your conscious constructive actions. You can also pump in some emotional gas through **SELF-EDUCATION**, avid reading ,and thoughtful information processing, Revelation does not come ready-made, or it can hardly be instilled by the best minds of the world. It is **a self-processed result** of feeling depleted of enthusiasm due to the turmoil of life and the internal wounds, inflicted by it. When the *electro-magnetic core of your personality gets demagnetized, you become wise.*

(Rule # 21 of Self-Renaissance)

To Be Inspired, Be Self-Inspiring!

2. Self-Gravity Formation

So, the book "Self-Renaissance" is *also an Auto-Suggestive inspirational self-programming guidebook* meant to re-program and re-condition the mind and crystalize your perception of where you are on the path of self-creation and why you are on it, or, in other words, help you accumulate the **SELF-GRAVITY** of a strong personality.

Most people are living in the chronic state of unawareness and confusion, stuck in fun-seeking and self-guilt trips tricking. So, the Inspirational Psychology for Self-Ecology is presented here as the formation of the self-gravity - the basis for mental balance and emotional equilibrium that we all need. With self-gravity, any impulsive action gets stopped by the " vigilant police" in the mind, commanding to you -H-A-L-T! You ground your negative impulses then and there.

Constant **SELF-CODING** with the help of *inspirational rhyming mind-sets* will reduce your impulsivity if you induct yourself with willpower, love and perseverance. You will be raising your self-consciousnesses that is the basic grader of your human value. *But there's no auto-suggestive programming without language-refining!* The direct line to self-consciousness is our language + intuition + conscience. Being in constant touch with the, you accumulate **PERSONAL GRAVITY** and make the right choice to either raise your self-consciousness or become dead in a living body. Your life depends on the way you operate your mind, language-wise.

Engaging your mind inspirationally, with an authoritative, characterful impact on it, you'll manage to accumulate your personal gravity and *get in touch with the universal energy -* the Super Consciousness that we've started tapping into digitally and that, in fact, is our **COMMON HUMAN SOUL** I which we are all One and inwardly related.

In God's Account, We All Count!

3. Self-Transformation with Elation!

As it is mentioned above, we cannot develop any Emotional Diplomacy Skills without ascending the self-transformational hills!

Never stop to radiate the light of a consciously built inner might!

Start with conducting the <u>Self-Assessment Meditation</u> and *X-raying yourself* every day in a general manner at the p*hysical, emotional ,mental, spiritual, and universal levels* (the book "The Best of Me Self-Image")

You will see what level you feel inadequate in. Any of the mind-sets taken from any of the seven books ,comprising *the Paradigm of Self-Renaissance,* consciously up-loaded into the file *Self-Resurrection*   of your smart- phone will act as your **CONSCIENCE ACTIVATOR** .

Practice mindful management of your emotions with conscience!

The present-day life demands a new, *conscious and conscientious personality type*   that fits the tough sci-tech reality and its incredible speed of life. To cope with the challenges, we need to create a new keyboard for managing our emotional make-up.

 It must be a <u>re-programmed memory storage,</u> a new Emotional Diplomacy compartment**, g**overned by the spirit-boosting mind-set:

<u>I'm my best friend; I'm my beginning and my end!</u>

Visit   the file every time the old habit comes to the surface, <u>pushing you to the impulsive reaction</u> that has always generated problems. I agree with *Dr. Dispenza* who says that jamming positive thoughts into the mind hoping that the positive reality will manifest is a utopia because *"people who try to think positively feel negative."* So, the Self-Ecology rule will code a negative move:

Be Aware of the Disrupting Emotion in Fact and Immediately Act!

4. Inspiration-Injected Gust Changes the Mood Very Fast!

I absolutely agree with the mind-set above because on the path of self-consciousness raising , our main action is to cultivate it in ourselves Never forget about your fractal establish **interconnectedness** of our inside and outside soul-redefining and soil-refining worlds, <u>engaging the heart and the mind in sync</u> for the solution of any problem that you face. The Super Consciousness is One with our souls; together, we are whole! You can do that by synergizing the main five elements, comprising the intellectually spiritualized fractal of your <u>emotionally grounded,</u> inwardly whole, and balanced Self.

<u>Body + Spirit + Mind + Self- Consciousness+ Super-Consciousness</u>

The climate of such synergy creates new self-awareness or new **SELF-WORTH ENERGY**, consciously generated in the process of the holistic self-creation. So, I see the purpose of the auto-suggestive or inductive self-programming that this book is based on in establishing the mediumship or inner synergy between mental-emotional **SELF-AWARENESS** and **INTITION** that is the soul's fruition. Intuition is innate in us, but it's in a dormant state. Intuition is our ability to look inside and beyond oneself at the cellular level. It's like listening to our inner population and hear their complaints or the approval of the actions that we take or are about to take. ***Intuition enables us to see the world beyond the boundaries of the reality.*** Our empirical perception of life is always putting us in touch with our Master Computer – God that helps us stay in the Mission's Bay!

So, it's Not that Important to ask now, "<u>How are You?</u>" It's much More Important to ask," <u>Why Are You?</u>"

5. Change Your Memory Operating System with the Auto-Suggestive Dictum!

At such moments, take your smart phone, open the file "*Self-Resurrection,*" find any elevating mind-set that resonates with your emotional state and induct it , controlling your breath while doing that. breathe in the first part of the self-induction, make a short pause, and say inwardly the second part of the induction, breathing out and <u>grounding the negativity that you have accumulated.</u>

AWARE ATTENTION paid to the negative emotion will help you stop the anger bite and establish the inner consensus inside! So, re-program your old emotional state to a new one with the help of the Active Auto-Suggestive Meditation.

SELF-MANAGEMENT means monitoring emotions consciously.

You will create new emotional rituals that will develop into new habits that will inevitably become *a newly conditioned response.* We all must be able to change the stale and out-worked convictions in our emotional and psychological framework ourselves! <u>Orchestrate your inner Self in every cell , going beyond yourself!</u> Self-rewind; Be One of a kind!

Use your smart phone as a digital psychological device , helping you to timely apply *the Auto-Suggestive Psychology for Self-Ecology.* Our present-day students know very little, if at all ,about psychology and the brain, and this simple. <u>Self-Help at Hand</u> will serve better than any visit to a psychologist because emotional help must be timely. Working auto-suggestively, *we do not generate unwanted consequences* that need much more time and character to be removed later with the overwhelming emotions of self-guilt that ruin the self-esteem. Auto-suggestively, we put the mind + heart healing link back in sync.

The Mind and Heart in Sync Form an Unbeatable Spiritual Link!

6. Let's Demystify the Know-How of Life's Normalcy to Thrive!

Don't be a victim of your conditioned Self. ***Reject, resist, and reform*** yourself again and again., visualizing your Self-Renaissance route each time you perform self-scanning and self-assessment in five dimensions of life holistically - *physical, emotional, mental, spiritual, and universal ..*

1) At the initial, ***mini level***, or the **physical management** of self-growth, gain the knowledge to consciously master the energy of the body in an orderly way thanks to new. **Self-Awareness.** Make physical maturation of judging yourself more important than judging others.

2) The ***meta level*** of our **emotional management** leaves much to be desired. The emotional intelligence is at the core of the Emotional Diplomacy Skills . So, **Self-Monitoring** as the next step of your self-growth must be focused on developing your personal gravity in life..

3) The third, ***mezzo level*** of **mental management**, called **Self-Installation** is the central one because knowledge gets up-dated every day, and your professional maturation depends on your self-awareness and emotional control skills. I suggest you master *ten essential vistas of intelligence. (See the Excellence Award winner " Living Intelligence or the Art of Becoming!" 2020))* to have a scientifically enhanced vision of life.) *"Everybody complains about the lack of money, no one complains about the lack of brains!"(Jewish wisdom)*

4) Next comes the ***macro-level*** - the level of **spiritual maturation** You need to acquire *"intellectualized spirituality"* as the goal of our existence on Earth and your full **Self-Realization** in life.

5) At the fifth, the ***super level*** of self-growth, **in the universal sense** you need to master order in life holistically, living in sync with the Universal Intelligence ,and ***realizing our exceptionality*** as the pay back to God for the gift of life, performing your **Self-Salvation.**

You Won't Ever Be Told about Your Imperfect Personal Mold!

7. The Trajectory of a Personality Formation

In sum, the **Holistic Self-Renaissance route** that I have outlined above must become the main incentive of your personality formation. *What do you think about yourself? Have you thought about the way people see you and perceive you?* <u>Do you agree with them? Why not?</u> I am sure that you have taken this book in your hands because *you know that you are very special,* but you have not yet arrived at the point when nothing can shake you in that opinion.

The *Auto-Suggestive programming* or **SELF-CODING** has helped many of my students become charismatic, outspoken, and personable Your self-awareness must become your mold of Self-Renaissance that keeps you in shape knowingly and consciously. Self-change is the hardest job on Earth.

But it is also the most rewarding one!

To do an **OBJECTIVE SELF-DISCOVERY** in five dimensions: *physical, emotional, mental, spiritual, and universal,* you must perform a thorough <u>selection and organization</u> of the good and bad qualities and ground those of them that are in the way of your personal renaissance. (*See "My Ode to Life" above*)

The way we program our cells determines who we will become because *we are the co-creators of ourselves,* not our DNA - <u>the matrix of our cells.</u> The Auto-Suggestive programming that I present briefly below will help you a lot on this path. only if your life-gaining is monitored with a conscious language <u>framing</u> because language is the executive power in our brains, and the way we frame our thoughts affects our being.

Auto-Suggestively Program Your Language-Speech Cell to Self-Excel!

Section 3

Thought-Obliqueness is in Managing Language Diplomacy Fitness!

There is no Auto-Suggestive Working if the Language is Broken!

"Words Change the DNA of Thought!"

(Ivonne Oswald)

"Language is a Physical Representation of Thought!" *(Leo Vygotsky)*

The Higher is Your Soul's Vibration, the Fuller is Your Self-Realization!

(Best Photos - Internet Collection)

Emotional Diplomacy is Rising on Your Language-Fitness Horizon!

1. To Self-Renaissance Succeed, Be Language-Fit!

To begin with, the process of putting your life in order in five circles of life (*physical, emotional, mental, spiritual ,and universal*) is being governed <u>at the universal level</u> of our merging with the Universal Consciousness that is enveloping us everywhere and that we technologically embrace now. If you are aware of ***the universal supervision***, you must establish a tight control over your thoughts and words that form them. <u>**Language shapes our intellectual landscape**</u>, and it determines our connection with the divine. ***"Language is the skin of the soul!"*** *(Fernando Lazaro Carreter)*

To stay in the right language behavior bay, think what you say!

So, self-growth must be constantly language controlled. We cannot beat our impulsivity and lack of emotional diplomacy unless we teach ourselves and our kids the **LANGUAGE DIPLOMACY SKILLS** and the structure of the ***Personality Matrix.***

<u>**Language Diplomacy is the Grammar of Self-Management!**</u>

Both are channeling us along the path of living holistically and consciously, in the inseparable unity of <u>**the form and content**</u> of our lives, constituting ***the fractals of intellectually spiritualized beings:***

Form + **Content**

(Body+ Spirit+ Mind) + **(Self-Consciousness + Universal Consciousness)**

Using curses, junk works, jargon, patterned thinking and engaging in meaningless chaotic talking <u>**disintegrates the mind and the body**</u> and negatively programs the cells, provoking different mind-body disorders.

Polluting Your Mind and Speech, You Become Evil-Bewitched!

2. Language-Fitness = Emotional Gravity

The world is still in the turmoil because for centuries, we haven't accumulated emotional intelligence, and we all lack **EMOTIONAL GRAVITY SKILLS** that are supposed to be instilled by <u>family education + academic education + self-education.</u> We need to eliminate our appalling ignorance in life and *start living with the personal gravity breading* that includes the formation of the best qualities of character <u>in five levels of self-growth</u>. The language in which we think and speak frames up our souls in the **FORM + CONTENT,** channeling the self-creation process psycho-linguistically. Language needs to be consciously controlled with respect to its grammatical correctness and lexical richness..

<u>So, develop Your Language Gravity without any Vanity!</u>

Super level	Super-Consciousness		Self-Salvation
Macro level	Self- Consciousness		Self-Realization
Mezzo level	Mind		Self- Installation
Meta level	Spirit		Self-Monitoring
Mini level	Body		Self-Awareness

Only enacting the *Emotional Diplomacy gravity restrictions* at any level of life consciously, can a person feel empowered to balance his / her emotions and *"reject, resist, and reform"* the evil impulsivity de-form

. **Being godly in a godless world means being language-refining!**.

Inner grace must be our <u>gravitational mechanism</u> at work, Self-Renaissance is impossible to be accomplished without language fitness established and emotional sickness, removed from the brain.

Your Sanity Must be Based on the Holistically Formed Personal Gravity!

3. Keep the Tongue in the Captivity of Your Mind's Run!

The phenomenon of the material nature of thought and the effect of our speech on it has been proven by a well-known German psycho-therapist *Dr. Nossrat Peseschkian* who states that "language is in unified relationship with mind and the psyche of a person."

His method demonstrates the detrimental effect of uncontrolled speech, full of junk words, slag and profanity, on the bodily health and the mind's sanity. Your Self-Ecology starts with controlling your emotional and psychic energy through speech.

Not to be speech-bewitched, make language is the portal of speech,

Obviously, the words that we voice out in an impulsive, irritated, angry speech of ours program our cells for sickness and mental disorders. The commonly used phrases - *I hate it! I can't take it anymore! Anyway. Shut up! It's crazy! What do I care! Damn it!* and, of course, the *"fricking fucking English"* in its numerous variations should be eliminated from your language. It shouldn't be negatively bewitched to destroy the perception switch. .*"I am responsible for what I say, but I am not responsible for what you hear."* (Oscar Wilde)

So, protect your soul from hyper emotions, exaggerated reactions, fake self-perception, lying, soul-twisting, impulsive responses, unwanted compromises, sensationalism, and random, quick-fix relationships that are ruined by instant gratification whim, pushing you on the road of self-corrode. *The mental-emotional equilibrium is vital for the cerebrum!* *So, say what we mean and mean what we say! Balance gets established* only with our thoughts, framed into the right words.

Auto-Linguistic Language Framing is the Psycho-Linguistic Life-Training!

4. Profanity Breaks the Soul's Sanity!

To remove your language sanity warts,

Get rid of the foul words!

Profanity breaks the soul,

And it breeds a sordid speech mole!

It gets rooted in the soul's soil,

And it steams your self-control boil!

The soil must be enriched with the mind's fertilizer,

And watered by the mouth-refined optimizer!

Then the soul will start speech sprouting

With kindness and goodness outing!

Finally, you'll grow the soul's console - garden

With your often visits into it, not sudden!

The soul's garden is your retreat,

You can be the Best of You in it!

Thus, your good speech will reform

The soul's language de-form!

And you'll be ready to proudly decree:

"My Language is Me!"

(Rule # 22 of Self-Renaissance)

Don't Say Everything You Know, but Know Everything You Say!

5. Don't Go Down the Road of Self-Corrode!

In sum, <u>our world is the materialization of our thoughts</u>, and the language is the main portal of these thoughts. A new branch of biology, medicine, physics, and bio-computing, called <u>Wave Genetics,</u> headed by a Russian scientist *P.P. Garayev* proves that *"our genome can create, transmit, and receive information generated by our cells at a quantum genetic level."*

An advanced American digital biologist, *Dr. Bruce Lipton*, writes, *"Every cell has its own energy-informational field that contains all the information about our past, present and future lives..* The DNA molecules exchange this information with the help of electro-magnetic waves that help the scientists create special genetic programs. It was thus discovered that *the DNA perceives human speech!* <u>Wow!</u> What we say, restructures our mental - emotional mind's bay!

Positive words stimulate the reserved energy reservoirs in the body, while the negative words and curses destroy the wave programs and immune reservoirs in it. So, don't get into the trap of being the slave of yourself and others that push your vulnerable buttons. *The Psychology for Self-Ecology* with *the Emotional Diplomacy* as its core is meant to help us in the accumulation of personal gravity and equanimity.

So, willfully, clean your sub-conscious emotional residue and boost your DNA energy with self-inspiration and self-reformation at the cellular level in the *physical, emotional, mental, spiritual, and universal* dimension of life. Doing the **SELF-SCANNING** and the auto-suggestive programming consciously, you will be uniting your cells into one universal link. *Anything that happens consistently gets linked!*

(Rule # 23 of Self-Renaissance)

Language Control Saves Your Soul!

Section 4

The Auto-Suggestive Meditation for Self-Inducted Elation!

Life-Elation

Starts with

Auto-Suggestive

Meditation!

*There are several examples of the **Auto-Suggestive Meditation** in my other books on Self-Resurrection. I present here just a few. As a matter of fact , any mind-set inducted consciously, <u>with language and breath control described here</u> acts as the **Active Auto-Suggestive Meditation** at hand..*

<u>Autosuggestibility is the Faith-Relationship with Yourself!</u>

(Rule # 24 of Self-Renaissance)

Form a Holistic Vision of Yourself in the World and the World in Yourself!

Self-Suggestibility is devoid of Doubt and Vanity Heritage.

Being Different is a Privilege!

1. Life-Gaining is in the Auto-Suggestive Self-Training!

Every one of us is "a complete electro-magnetic system" *(Nikola Tesla)* that gets plugged into a positive or negative informational circuit. If we violate the ethic laws, **we get plugged into the anti-world** that we perceive as the devil. As the result, the informational channels, the chakras, partially or wholly, become closed, and we get punished at the cellular level. You are the President of your cell population, and your addressing cells auto-suggestively determines the state they will be in.

According to modern physics, *(The Theory of the Physical Vacuum" / Dr. G.I. Shipov)* we have a " *functional bi-directional torsion field system of communication",* and when we think negatively, we are forming the negative "*torsion fields*" that are enveloping us, creating*" the negatively energized phantoms"* around us. So, we must ground the negative thoughts and program ourselves for the constructive inner change, changing the electro-magnetic charge around the brain with the authoritative, inspirational work of the mind. It is vitally important on the path of self-creation because we can master the aware tuning of the **AUTO-ANTENNA** and thus, synchronize the brain + mind work and .mind+ heart conscious connection.

The reminder: It is also the path of raising your self-consciousness in all five levels integrally - *physically + emotionally + mentally + spiritually + universally.* Talking in terms of the energy centers - **chakras**, we need to integrate all the seven charkas *or the centers of consciousness,* to attain Christ's Consciousness in the future. Thus, hopefully, the humanity will reach **the Gold Age** on our evolutionary stem in some unanswerable when. *(See the book" Self-Taming" / 2020).*

Be the President of Your Cell Population. Keep Them in Elation!

2. Envision the Structure of Self-Renaissance

It is an accepted fact that it is much easier to say, *"Stay away from the poison of life!"* *(Carl Yung)* than actually do it. To be successful in accomplishing this very challenging goal, we must first learn to resist the temptation and then *to magnetize our inner core with new values.* "**Resist, reject, and reform!**" *(Rav. P.S .Berg)*

In the celestial terms, to change the evil inside, a badly willed side of you into a divine one, is the most challenging thing that needs **conscious mind-reprogramming.**

We need to reverse *the triple 666*, signifying **sex – heart - mind** to the life - defining unity of *the triple 999 –* **mind + heart + sex.** When interviewed once, *Nikola Tesla* asked the journalist to always note that " *he played his life himself and enjoyed keeping it from evil.*" So, play a solo role in your life's concert, too.

Form + Content = a New You! (666 ⟶ 999)

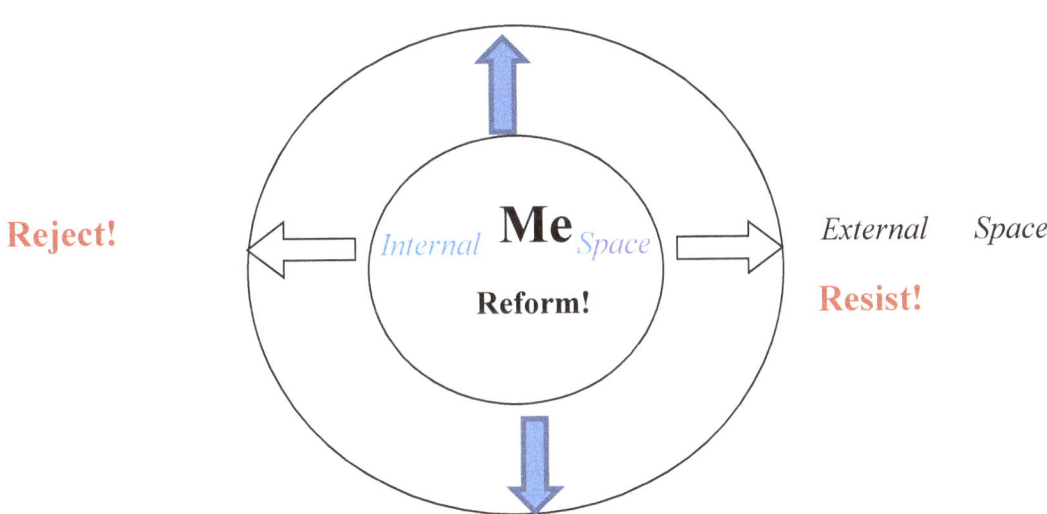

If you feel lazy or resistant to do any action, start counting backwards, *commanding to your subconscious mind to follow the conscious mind's lead.* **Authoritative self-suggesting develops aware attention and strengthens the willpower.** You will manage to resist the impulsivity that dumbs you down.

"Three, two, One - Go! or Five, Four, Three, Two, One - Go!"

3. Strengthen Your Magnetic Gene with the Self-Suggestive Hygiene!

Super level	Super-Consciousness	Self-Salvation
Macro level	Self- Consciousness	Self-Realization
Mezzo level	Mind	Self- Installation
Meta level	Spirit	Self-Monitoring
Mini level	Body	Self-Awareness

The five-dimensional nature of Self-Renaissance *must be grounded in your inner space* – your **HEART** and *envisioned in the outer space* - your **MIND** . The **cross-like magnetic core** of your personality is in the **(- 0 +)** mathematical proportion. Instill the auto-inductive mind-sets, visualizing the stage you're *working on in time* (*the vertical vector*) *and in space* (*the horizontal vector.*)

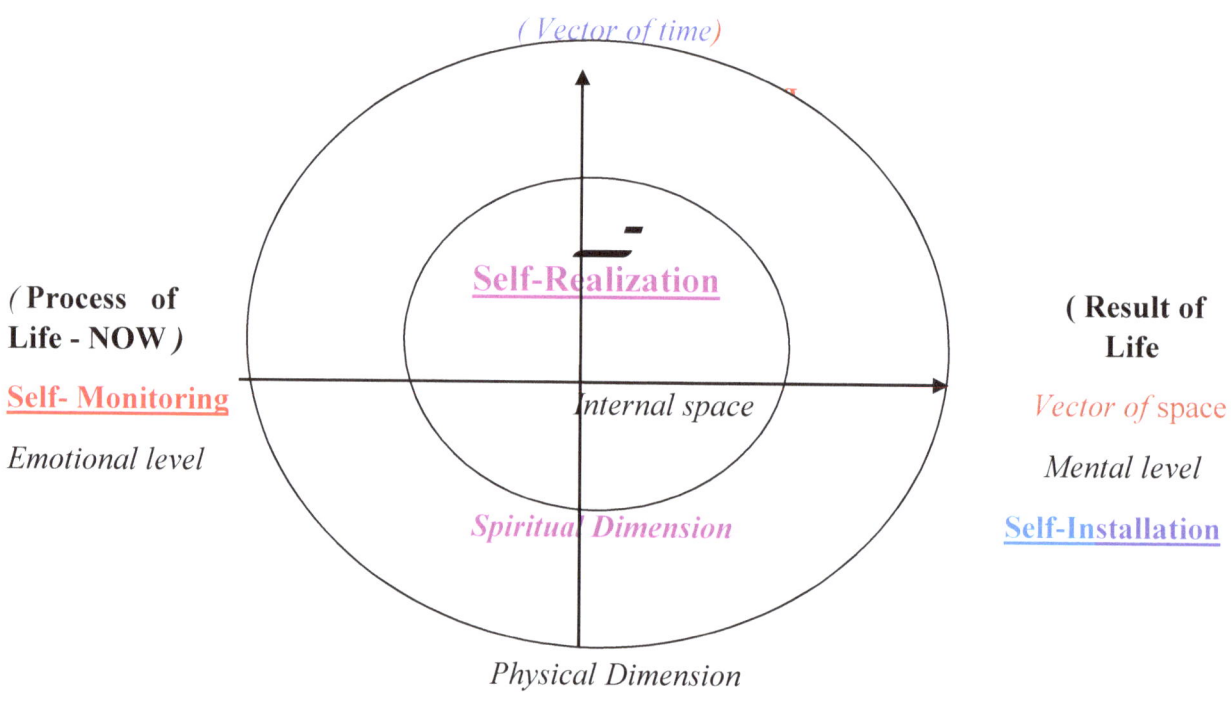

Self-Salvation *Universal Dimension /* **Future**

(Vector of time)

Self-Realization

(Process of Life - NOW)

Self- Monitoring

Emotional level

Internal space

(Result of Life

Vector of space

Mental level

Self-Installation

Spiritual Dimension

Physical Dimension

Self-Awareness */ Physical level /* **Past**

Living Intelligence in Action Fixes Your Inner Fraction

4. Become Wise and Feel God-Supervised!

Coming back to the inspirational purpose of this book, *the auto-suggestive inspirational back-up* is needed first because it is based on constant **SELF-CONTROL** that is paramount for your self-creation as self-reflection. It's the time of your establishing a conscious connection with the Universal Intelligence while you're doing your **SELF-SCANNING.**

a) *To begin with*, you must establish control over your universal goal. It must be prompted to you by your exceptionality, your uniqueness, granted to you from the Above. The aim of education is to help a student discover his / her exceptionality as early as possible and make its realization the goal of life. No market demands should count here

b) Next, be committed to your spiritual values and *have an unshakable faith* in yourself and your exceptionality the realization of which becomes your mission in life

c) *Enrich your intelligence* by sifting the information that you get for its validity and then storing it in your brain at the mental level;

d) *Harness your extreme emotions* to pursue the *Emotional Diplomacy rules* that you need to work out for yourself in the emotional realm;

e) Finally, never lose sight of your physical might. Keep your body healthy and whole; it physically embraces your soul.

Also, governing yourself "*from the Above* " means to never forget that the piercing eyes of your spiritual leader whose messages you are following are always on you, and *this supervision encompasses all five levels of your self-growth*, *from bottom to top and from top to bottom_ (See "Self-Taming"/2020)* Be sure to realize that spiritual maturation is your Self-Salvation from the commonality of thinking, speaking, feeling ,and acting. Be God and self-guided in the mind Be One of a kind!

God is the Testing Force of Your Self-Worth!

5. *"The Best is Yet to Come!"* (Carolyn Leigh)

It's essential to conduct *Active Auto-Suggestive meditations (see below)* as often as you can, starting with the Universal level of self-transformation and conducting self-inducting or self-coding after scanning yourself holistically and objectively at each stage

Keep doing the auto-suggestive work everywhere and at any time to boost your spirit, elevate the mood, and enthuse your mind for pro-active, not reactive actions. The auto-suggestive Self-Resurrection file in your smart phone should be organized in the same orderly way- *physical, emotional, mental, spiritual and universal levels.*

There won't be any depression after the Auto-Suggestive session!

Meditation is our direct connection with the Universal Intelligence - God. Only when we see ourselves from inside out, can we become balanced and whole. Get into the habit of meditating every free minute and program your cells for health, love, and success with *the Auto-Suggestive zest.* The language purity comes to the surface here. Language is shaping the mind and our emotional rewind.

We'll soon have the robots, acting as our best friends, and I hope *they will be monitoring us in these five dimensions,* reminding us of the mind-sets that rhyme because " *the rhyming word goes best inward."*

You might want to make up your own boosters, but they must rhyme, too. Precede doing it, roaming through all the rest parts of the book in sync with the Universal Intelligence that governs your transformation all the time. It's great to do it before going to sleep, after you have scanned yourself in five levels in a general way. *Feel happy and content on the path of willful self-bend!*

Have the Auto-Suggestive File as Your Psychological Self-Help at Hand.

6. Explore Yourself More and More; That's the Self-Transformation Law!

An Active Auto-Suggestive meditation is very simple, *"but the simplest things are the hardest to accomplish."(Nicola Tesla)* It is meant to help you build up your Emotional Diplomacy Skills first, at least in the dilettante way. Such self -programming can also be used to fix your spirit, if need be. The process of *Self-Resurrection in five realms of life* is very important for self-organization because it develops the skill of self-scanning and self-refining with the help of self-inductions that program your mind unpretentiously and very beneficially in *physical, emotional, mental, spiritual, and universal strata of life.*

All over the world, in every culture and language, people use the quotes from the sacred books, different proverbs and sayings that add wisdom to their life experience. We all learn them from our grandparents, parents, friends, etc. and they always help us assess the situation or just sound smart. Many sayings rhyme, too, and we easily retrieve them from the memory to qualify our actions in an exact way. Autosuggestibility does the same to the mind. It's a back-up for your mind, mood, and psyche.

The rhyming mind-sets are memory friendly. They are also technologically friendly if you upload them into a smart phone and use them to boost yourself for a constructive action, or just to change the mood that might sag for whatever reason. Just pick a mind-set of your choice and induct it with the help of your conscious breathing. *Breathe in,* inwardly saying the first part of the induction, make a pause to instill it in the mind and the heart, and *say / think* of the second part of the induction while breathing out. Ground your negativity with it.

. Be a Conscious Humankind - One with the Universal Mind!

7. Self-Suggestibility is the Stage of the Self-Synthesis!

To round off your holistic self-channeling in five levels integrally and auto-suggestively, constantly check and balance your life's pendulum or <u>the fractal connection of all the aspects of your being.</u>

Body + Spirit + Mind + Self- Consciousness+ Super-Consciousness

Your work on this unity must be monitored by the evolutionary paradigm (Synthesis -Analysis -Synthesis) that will help you X-ray yourself inwardly. Emotional Diplomacy Skills get formed in the mind by way of your conducting regular self-scanning inwardly and privately.

<u>Step One</u> - Start with <u>Self-Synthesis</u> - the general assessment of your day and you in it holistically. Give yourself an objective grade

<u>Step Two</u> – Continue reviewing your day with <u>Self-Analysis</u> in five levels - *physical, emotional, mental, spiritual, universal.*

Step Three -Complete your self-revision with the final <u>Self-Synthesis</u> in its integral fractal unity. See if you can change the grade.

Having diagnosed yourself holistically, ***do the self-programming,*** using the mind-set that you have stored in the smart phone or memorized and that is up-lifting your spirit best in such situation The inspirational boosters that make up this book are kind of dictated to me from the Above.

It's weird, but true. I just have an inspiring concept hit my mind, and I jot it down immediately to later boost my own spirt, my students,' or my life-overwhelmed friends. Upload into your brain the mind-sets that resonate with you most. Pay attention to <u>the correctness of the language</u> to conduct the auto-suggestive programming.

Autosuggestibility is in Our Genes; It's the Emotional Diplomacy Means!

8. Make Suggestibility Your Main Mood-Changing Ability!

The Maxwell's second law of thermodynamics, otherwise known as **the Law of Entropy**, continues to dominate our lives, leading to our dis-integration and dis-connection from birth Everything in life is subject to the rules of entropy *unless we establish a proper guidance over ourselves.* Tap into the telephone line of the Universe and be your own boss! *Meditate as often as you can to appease your cells' clan.*   *"Be done with the stone-age attitude to yourself!" (Dr. Joe Dispenza)*

"A human body is like a tree. Its trunk is the spine that is channeling the two energy torrents – **the first one**, coming from space and **the second one,** coming from the Earth. *The two channels are the two vectors of life.* *(See Chunk 3 above)* Live in a tandem and unity with them *"We need to consciously operate these torrents that are supplying us with the energy, or the prana of life." (Dmitriy Vereshchagin*)

By the vector of time *(up)* , we breathe in health, success, love ,and wealth. Making a pause, we instill them in the conscious mind *by the vector of space* . Breathing out, (*down*) we're grounding sickness, failure, etc., leaving them in the past.

Do this **ACTIVE AUTO-SUGGESTIVE** programming looking at the Sun and breathing in and out its golden energy, Do the **Alternative Breathing.** Close your right nostril with a thumb, breathe in the first part of any induction through the left open nostril (*men should starts breathing with the right nostril).* M*ake a pause, focusing your attention on the heart* and breathe out the second part of the induction through the right nostril, closing the left one with the pointing finger. *Make a pause to instill the induction in your conscious mind.* Now, breathe in through the right , open nostril, closing the left nostril with the pointing finger. Do the same three times.

Life in - Death out! / Light in - Darkness out! Health in- Sickness out! / etc.

9. The Basic Self-Induction

All my books have the mind-sets that conceptually illustrate this or that dimension of self-growth. Among all of them, there is one that I present as the **BASIC AUTO-INDUCTION** that will become your <u>self-help device</u> in any situation, be it a romantic enrolment, a family problem, or a job misunderstanding.

<u>Instead of being reactive, become consciously pro-active!</u>

There are very many self-inductions in other books, too, and you, for sure, have singled out some of them for yourself. Great! I am glad you find them helpful. The one below has been first mentioned as the basic one in the Excellence award winning book on personality formation” *Living Intelligence or the Art of Becoming!”* As a matter of fact, it I has been <u>the self-inductive   tool</u> for my students for years, and it is the one I rely on myself. It will be handy as *your* **psychological back-up,** or <u>a self-hypnosis helping hand.</u>

It is very simple, but extremely effective because it is easily memorized and character-molding, **reminding you of your exceptionality** and the necessity to prove it with your actions.. It has helped hundreds of my students on the path of intelligence-formation, career building, and Self-Installation. It is also very effective to conduct *the Suggestive Meditation,* one of which I describe below.

I know who I am!

<u>I am a strong, calm, and determined owner of my firm will!</u>

I can do   *(say whatever you need to do)*

I want to …;

And I will…!

I’m becoming better and better, healthier and healthier, kinder and kinder
with each breath, each coming moment, day, months, year).

(You need to regulate your breathing. Breathe in while inducting the first part of each statement in this formula. **Make a short pause while instilling it into the conscious mind.** *Breathe out, when inwardly saying the second part of the statement.) Relax to fix it in.*

To Be Never Upset, Change Your Mind-Set!

10. Keep Changing the Memory Operating System with the Auto-Suggestive Dictum!

Reminder: At an upsetting moment, take your smart phone again, open the file "*Self-Resurrection,*" find any elevating mind-set that resonates with your emotional state and induct it, *controlling your breath while doing that*. Breathe in the first part of the self-induction, make a short pause+, focusing your **AWARE ATTWNTION** on the heart, and say inwardly the second part of the induction, breathing out , grounding the negativity that you have accumulated.

Awareness helps us stop the anger bite and establish the inner consensus inside! So, re-program your old emotional state to a new one with the help of active programming or re-programming during the *Active Auto-Suggestive meditation*. You will create new emotional mind+ heart rituals that will develop into new habits that will inevitably become new conditioned conscious responses.

We all must be able to change the stale and out-worked convictions in our emotional and psychological framework ourselves! Our present-day students know very little if at all about psychology and the brain , and this simple *Self-help at Hand* stops impulsivity and helps better than a later visit to a psychologist because emotional help must be timely. Working auto-suggestively, you do not generate unwanted consequences that need much more time and character to be deleted.

A specialist's help is a need, but self-help is a fit!

The consciously monitored mind+ heart connection will heal your impersonality, indifference, and brutality and form the **EMOTIONAL DIPLOMACY GRAVITY!** .

The Auto-Suggestive Link Puts the Mind + Heart Back in Sync.

11. Exude the Emotional Diplomacy Mood!

Let me go over some points again here. Always, in any unpleasant situation, remember: **Emotional Diplomacy is your Aristocracy!** Put yourself together inwardly, *synchronizing your self-consciousness with the Universal Consciousness* through your intuition and conscience.

One-sidedness of our professional education must be holistically re-structure to bridge the gap of ignorance in Psychology and neuroscience. **The knowledge of Psychology and the brain is life-gaining!** We all need the support of self-worth and self-sustainability. Having the file " *Self-Resurrection*" in your smartphone or any book on self-creation at hand will help your eyes catch the mind-set that will boost your spirit then and there.

You might want to make up the self-boosting mind-sets of your own, but they must be rhyming and easily memoizable. The inspirational auto-suggestive-injecting will imbue you with more willpower to confront any situation because it is **self-awareness + life awareness** charged. " Just the mind-set,

Life is tough, but I'm tougher!" does the trick.

Most importantly, such self-boosting will fill up your subconscious mind with *special schemes that pulsate at higher vibrational frequencies*, helping you get rid of the schemes of anger, hate, lying, and fear. Inspiring yourself auto-suggestively, you make yourself invulnerable to petty sarcasm, rudeness, envy, and aggression. Keep inducting yourself with:

I Can do it. I want to do it. And I will do it!

In fact, **auto-suggestibility is the final stage of Self-Synthesis** because self-boosting should be instilled in the mind at the final stage of Self-Synthesis that must always follow the evolutionary paradigm -

Self-Synthesis – Analysis – Self Synthesis!

12. Exceptionality and Self-Gravity

In sum, *the Active Auto-Suggestive Meditation* will instill in the brain the holistic philosophical principle- synthesis - analysis-synthesis for life. Apply this principle to any aspect of your everyday life - doing home chores, cooking, solving business problems or grounding conflicts in relationships, etc. Using Auto-suggestive programming consciously, you'll get into the habit of conducting ob**jective SELF-SCANNING:**

Who you are;	How you are;	and	Why you are!
Self-Synthesis	⟶ *Self-Analysis*	⟶	*Self- Synthesis*
Self-Generalize	**Self- Internalize**		**Self-Actualize**!

Any gifted person who is committed to realizing his / her exceptionality in life ***must have personal gravity*** that is based on ***the Earth gravitation support***, on the one hand, and establishing the sync with the positive / negative charges of the Universal Consciousness Field, on the other. This double support is possible with mind-controlled breathing.

Self-Synthesis - *Breathe in* the first half of any self-induction.

Self-Analysis - **M**ake a pause, ***focusing your attention in the heart*** and instill this part of the mind-set in the conscious mind. Your **AUTO-ANTENNA** must be tuned into the mind + heart link.

Self-Synthesis - *Breathe out* the second part of the mind-set, uniting inwardly the heart and the mind in a new, holistic and positively inductive way and ground the worst of your thoughts, words, feelings. and actions. Self-Synthesis must be concluded with the mind-set below that you need to boost your self-esteem..

(Rule # 25 of Self-Renaissance)

I'm My Best Friend (breathe in) – Pause in the heart - I'm My Beginning and + My End! (breathe out)

13. "The Spirit and the Soul are Common Consciousness." (G.W. Leibniz "-Philosophy of Mind)

Thus, the **Inspirational Psychology for Self-Ecology** will put you in the fractal unity of (body + spirit + mind + self- consciousness + super-consciousness). The fractal Unity is an integrated presentation of the soul!

1) In the physical dimension, (body), you'll conceptualize *self-awareness, kindness, and compassion.* / stage - Self-Awareness

2 In the emotional realm (spirit), you'll develop the *emotional equilibrium, love, and the attitude of gratitude.* / stage – Self-Monitoring

3) At the mental stage (mind), you'll focus on *order, intelligence, and a professional installation.* / stage – Self-Installation

4) The spiritual advancement stage (self-consciousness) will direct you to personable perfection and *spiritual growth, based on spiritualized intelligence and forgiveness.* / stage - Self-Realization

5) The universal realm of self-growth (super-consciousness) is crowned with *the completion of your mission on Earth and full realization of your exceptionality* that goes beyond the limits of the possible into the materialization of the impossible. / stage – Self-Salvation

Do the self-inducting or auto-programming of your cells selectively, depending on your **physical, emotional, mental spiritual, and universal** needs, in a conscious and natural way, without obligating yourself. Make the synchronization of the heart+ mind link a regular, natural, spontaneous, and pleasant action. The Auto-Suggestive relaxation is contagious! The healing modality of your mind leads to the healing modality of the brain, the spirit, and the body. Be self-aware of your fractal wholeness !" *Being whole makes you holy!"* (Deepak Chopra)

Establish Interconnectedness at Every Level of Your Self-Renascence!

Part Three of the Book

(Synthesis - Analysis - Synthesis structure of the book)

Life Essence is

in Five Stages of

Self-Renaissance

(Final Synthesis)

(The Illustration of the Philosophy above in five dimensions

of Self-Reissuance)

(Rule # 26 of Self-Renaissance)

"Seek and You Will Find" if You Unite

the Heart, the Spirit, and the Mind!

Accept the Gift to the Present-Day Universal Shift; Self-Uplift!

Self-Salvation

Universal dimension

Super-Consciousness

Self-consciousness

Self-Realization

Spiritual *dimension*

Mind

Self-Installation

Mental dimension

Spirit

Self-Monitoring

Emotional dimension

Body

Self-Awareness

Physical dimension

(The sacred mountain Machapuchare , worshiped as the Home of God Shiva, Nepal)

Life is Synchronized with the Grandeur Before Your Eyes!

1. Develop New Clarity and Self-Gravity!

It's vital for us to consciously install a new, fractal **SELF-GRAVITY** in the mind to synchronize the inner Self.

(Body + Spirit + Mind) + (Self-Consciousness + Universal Consciousness)

This symbiosis controls our thoughts and forms the **SELF-WORTH GRAVITY** of an individual's value as <u>a new time generated matrix of a personality,</u> simple in form, but complex .in its content. It presents the "**SIMPLEXITY**" of the paradigm of self-creation *in its five main stages.* Like five fingers on the right hand , put into a fist and turned into the horizontal position as they do it in the Martial Arts, get charged with the energy of the entire body by putting all five circles of your life together into one **SELF-WORTH** sync. You'll mentally hit any problem in <u>your inner synergy state</u>. Thus, you will be standing solidly on the path of **SELF-RENAISSANCE**. If you envision these stages and monitor your life toward their holistic unity, you'll become unbeatable and unstoppable in the realization of your exceptionality.

<u>Mental Clarity charges Self-Gravity!</u>

Self-Awareness $\Longleftrightarrow$ **Self-Monitoring** $\Longleftrightarrow$ **Self-Installation**- $\Longleftrightarrow$ **elf-Realization** $\Longleftrightarrow$ **Self-Salvation!**

Please, note, that I only outline this huge lump of knowledge, presenting the paradigm of *Self-Renaissance* as a complete holistic system on the path of self-creation because *I'm sure of the objective value of this system.* It can always be re-filled with new knowledge that will not compromise the system. <u>There is no system without the structure!</u> You must fill up your digitized mind with live cells ready to unwind the double helix of an animal DNA into the

Five-Dimensional Star of Your Self- <u>Renaissance Display!</u>

2. Raise the Magnitude of Your Self-Renaissance Attitude!

The Reminder - To monitor your *Self-Renaissance* inwardly and outwardly, conduct constant self-refining, starting with the initial **Self-Synthesis** when you synthesize the notion of yourself in the first level – 1.**Self-Awareness-** getting to know your exceptional goal in life

Next, you should perform **Self-Analysis** (*stages 2,3,4. below*), X-raying **objectively** the three aspects of life (*emotional, mental, spiritual*) in which you acknowledge becoming a better or worse human being.

2. **Self-Monitoring** – (the book " *Soul-Refining!*")

3. **Self-Installation**—(*"Living Intelligence or the Art of Becoming!"*)

4. **Self-Realization** – (the book -" *Self-Taming!)*

5) The final **Self-Synthesis** is concluded with the stage **Self-Salvation**, synthesizing your collective notion of self-growth in sync with other levels of self-resurrection. Conducting **SELF-ASSESSMENT** by the paradigm **Self-Synthesis - Self-Analysis -Self-Synthesis** daily, weekly, monthly, and yearly, you will master yourself holistically and your *Self-Renaissance* will become a reality. You don't need to read all the books. Just choose the level you need a back-up in most.

This book starts with *the fifth level of Self-Salvation* because our present-day digital connection to the Universal Intelligence allows us to supervise our self-growth digitally, literary everywhere, having the smart phone, uploaded with the **SELF-HELP MIND-SETS** at hand. Artificial intelligence in sync with human intelligence (*the effect of Singularity)* is doing its magic exponentially now. **WOW!** That's why our present-day times need people with well-trained, fundamentally cultured, and technologically aware self-consciousness.

Life is the Journey to Yourself!

3. The Structure of the Holistic Psycho-Culture (*Synthesis* - *Analysis* - *Synthesis*)

Inspirational Psychology for Self-Ecology!

(The Illustrative Part of the book , presenting five stages of Self-Renaissance)

Self-Salvation - *The universal life circle* -**Final Synthesis**

Self-Realization- *The spiritual life circle* – **Analysis**

Self-Installation - *The mental life-circle*- **Analysis**

Self-Monitoring- *The emotional life circle*- **Analysis**

Self -Awareness- *The physical life-circle* - **Initial Synthesis**

Self-Synthesis ⟹ **Self-Analysis** ⟹ **Self-Synthesis!**

(Self-Awareness) ➡ *(Self-Monitoring + Self-Installation +Self-Realization)* ➡*(Self-Salvation)*

Being Conscious Today Means Consciously Monitoring the Reality *Universally, Spiritually, Mentally, Emotionally, and Physically.*

4. Five Stages of Self-Renaissance and the Basic Mind-Sets, illustrating Them

(From top to bottom)

Stage Five - *Universally directed Self-Renaissance* - <u>SELF-SALVATION</u>

1. Go Beyond, Fully Beyond, Completely Beyond!

Stage Four-- *Spiritually directed Self-Renaissance* — <u>SELF-REALIZATION</u>

2. I Can Roam Any Terrain with God in My Vein!

Stage Three -*Mentally directed Self-Renaissance* — <u>SELF-INSTALLATION</u>

3. Intellectualize Your Heart and Emotionalize the Mind.

Stage Two - *Emotionally directed Self-Renaissance* -<u>SELF-MONITORING</u>

4. Life - Gaining is in Self-Taming!

Stage One - *Physically directed Self-Renaissance* — <u>SELF-AWARENESS</u>

5. <u>Be Self-Governable, Not Mass Media Programmable!</u>

Mind it please, ***there's no necessity to read the book consequentially.*** Each of the stages features the level of life that you might want to give a boost to. ***The conceptual structure*** of the book is based on the page-long chunks of information, *retaining the structure inside the structure*, as the Russian Dolls do. Construct your own Self-Help text and refresh your moral values and beliefs.

Self-Gravity is the basis for our Mental-Emotional Sanity!

Review any stage of the book that reflects the weakest aspect of your life at that moment. <u>**Program your cells with the new mind-sets!**</u> Upload them into your smart phone and instill them into your mind. through conscious breathing. Thus, you'll remove your ***sub-conscious stereotyped thinking*** and create your own **Universal Intelligence linking** that will help you ground the unwanted habits and beliefs and stay on the path of Self-Renaissance eternally.

Commit to Being Self-Renaissance Fit!

5. Accept My Well-Wishing on the
Journey to Self-Renaissance.

I invite you to optimize your journey consciously, inspirationally, and holistically.

I hope that in leafing further through the pages of the five
main Auto-Suggestive stages of the book -

(universal, spiritual, mental, emotional, and physical),

your life inspiration and self-transformation

will be ignited in you that otherwise

might not have been kindled.

"Things are getting worse and better at the same time now."

(Eckhart Tolle)

We need to put ourselves together to face the new reality.

Body + Spirit + Mind + Self-Consciousness + Universal Consciousness

= Self- Acculturation + Self Gravity!

So, sharpen and focus your Aware Attention to get to the

Self-Renaissance Dimension!

Bon Voyage!

Stay Aboard! Tune Yourself up to the
<u>Universal Station God</u>!

(Best Photos – the Internet Collection)

"Atheism is the Communist Defeatism!"

(Sergey Esenin, a great Russian poet)

Stage Five

(Self-Monitored Stage for a Self-Salvation Sage)

Universally

Guided

Self-Renaissance

Eternity is What's Ahead for those who Can Self-Reset!

Our Common Life Essence is in the Universal Renaissance!

Self-Renaissance is the Faith-Relationship with God!

Universal Intelligence is Objective.

It is God-Driven!

Self-Culture Means Holistically Based Self-Acculturation!

Self-Renaissance

Form   +   Content

(Body+ Spirit+ Mind) + (Self-Consciousness + Universal Consciousness)

Living Intelligence   + Enlightened Self-Consciousness = A Whole Self!

- - - - - - - - - - - - - - - - - -

5. *Universal Realm = Self- Acculturated;*

4. *Spiritual Realm = Self- Realized!*

3. *Mental Realm = Self-Educated;*

2. *Emotional Realm = Self-Controlled;*

1. *Physical Realm = Self-Aware*

The Harmony of the Heart + Mind Sync is the Main Goal of the Emotional + Mental link =

Personal Gravity = Raised Self-Consciousness

The process of raising Self-Consciousness is very complicated and must be consciously monitored by everyone of us, willing to upgrade their physical, emotional, mental, spiritual, and universal status in life.

The New Culture of Self-Acculturation is in

Self-Consciousness Formation.

Section 1

(Self-Salvation Stage of a Self-Renaissance Sage)

Your Exceptionality Grows in the

Universal Infinity!

Intelligence, sacredness, love, kindness, compassion ,nobility, aristocratism, health and grace

come from space!

We are all walking in faith, in hope ,and with love,

through the power of the Omnipresent God in our cells and in everything around us.

(Rule # 27 of Self-Renaissance)

Practice Noble Silence, Personal Gravity , and Normalcy. It's Universal Diplomacy!

We're all being watched from the
God's Universal Porch.

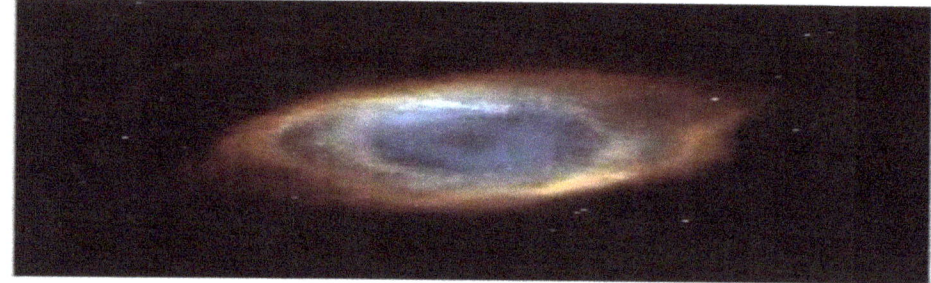

Эта фотография — очень редкая, а само событие случается раз в три тысячи лет.
Это фото уже свершило чудеса во многих жизнях.
Задумай желание... ты видишь Око Божие.
Это точно: ты увидишь перемены в своей жизни в течение дня.
Поверь, не храни этот э-мэйл у себя.
Отправь его, по крайней мере, 7 людям.
Эта фотография снята НАСА телескопом Хаббл.
Она называется: "ОКО БОЖИЕ"

Слишком невероятно погасить его.

Пошли это фото своим друзьям и увидишь, что будет.

This is the photo made by **the Telescope Hubble.** *It's called* " **The God's Eye.**" ***Edwin Hubble***, the astronomer, demonstrated that the Universe was indeed expanding with galaxies moving away from one another.

The Universe is dynamic, continually expanding and contracting, like everything in the Universe, starting ***from mini to super levels of existence*** , with our hearts working in unison with its vibrations, too. There is the Informational Field around the Earth, and it has its own Data Base, connected to the Universal Field accordingly.

Be Aware of That and Stay Connected.
Disconnection is Death!

1. God's Brain is One!

In the Universal Life Span,

God's Brain is One!

> *Every galaxy and constellation*
>
> *Are His formation!*

We are One in His brain,

We are unique in His domain!

> *But our religious vision*
>
> *Is not His provision.*

We do not choose to be black, yellow, or white,

So why do we fight?

> *Why don't we abstract*
>
> *From the centuries of this whack?*

Let's reverse

The perception of the human moths!

> *Let's rewind*
>
> *The history of our collective human mind*

And Unite as One Cell

In the Vast Universal spell!

We Complete Our Mission on Earth at the Universal Level of Self-Growth.

2. Our New Spiritual Volume

The Universal dimension of our life is life-determining for us because it encompasses all the rest dimensions of life, channeling our evolution in the right direction.

As human beings, we can create images, dictated to us by our imagination connected to the Universal Informational Field. Our universal existence generates these images and helps our brains to evolve in this direction, *planting the evolutionary ideas in the heads of* the most inquisitive and knowledge-seeking of us.

Then these images, as the incredible ideas, prompted to us from the Above **get realized in the material reality** thanks to the effort and dedication of their owners. It's well acknowledged that the most advanced ideas come to the heads of different people in the world, but only beyond the terrestrial ones bring them to reality.

The universal changes are huge now, and they embrace every area of our **TECHNOLOGICALLY MONITORED** lives. The human brain started perceiving new vibrations and much more subtle frequencies impact every aspect of our life - *physically, emotionally, mentally, spiritually, and universally,* creating new, *spiritually more intellectualized and more inwardly integrated fractals* of new human beings with a technologically enhanced **SELF-GRAVITY.**

Form + **Content**

(Body+ Spirit+ Mind) + **(Self-Consciousness + Universal Consciousness)**

Living Intelligence + Enlightened Self-Consciousness = Personal Gravity!

We are living at the time now when the form and the content of our lives are monitored by technology that is making the unconsciously going with the flow ones just human robots with no mental, psychological , or emotional gravity.

Realize Your Exceptionality with a New, Self-Monitored Personal Gravity!

3. Self-Renaissance is Creating a New Self-Universe!

Obviously, our self-consciousness is evolving towards a much higher, more noble, and the mass media free self-consciousness that is creating in us a new, present life aware **SPIRITUAL VOLUME.** It means that religion and science are still in defiance, and our religiously dogmatic and limitedly divisive vision of the world must be gradually changing to *a more physically, emotionally, mentally, and spiritually inclusive one.*

We are becoming technologically united at present .

As a result, a new, holistic human matrix is shaping us for the creation of a **NEW SELF-UNIVERSE,** the universe of a free personality that is re-establishing the <u>heart + mind</u> unity lost in the turmoil of life.. More people are applying new knowledge for self-growth and life improvement and discover their God-given **EXCEPTIONALITY.** <u>So, stop being a victim of the collective dictum!</u> The changes inside and outside are enormous and exponential. We need to embrace them holistically and whole-heartedly, establishing an unbreakable connection with *the Master Mind* that is governing us on this new, digitally enhanced evolutionary stratum of life. To be wise and totally self-realized, therefore, you need *to internalize the new knowledge, analyze, individualize , and strategize* it on the path of achieving your exceptional goal. Finally, you will have to <u>externalize</u> your personality in implementing it and accomplishing full *Self-Realization* in life.

Internalize - Analyze - Personalize – Strategize - Externalize!

4. Self-Ecology Starts with Your Exceptionality Geology

The Universal Dimension of life is the most vital one for us since it is governing us in every cell that in vibrating in unison with the Super-Consciousness enveloping us everywhere. Therefore, the actions that are enlightened by self-consciousness are constructive; while the actions that are done unconsciously are always disruptive.

We should be modelling our life with the clear awareness of the Universal gift of life granted to us from the Above**.** And your goal in life must be based on the conscious realization of <u>**your exceptionality**</u> - the inner urge to make the world better by realizing this unique gift holistically, in five stages of self-growth - *physical, emotional ,mental, spiritual, universal. (* <u>*www.language-fitness.com*</u> */ section Self-Resurrection).*

(Self-Awareness)➡ *(Self-Monitoring + Self-Installation +Self-Realization)* ➡ *(Self-Salvation)*

Like zillions of shapeless and meaningless rocks on the ocean beach, you must be the one that stands out and attracts attention with its **INNER DESIGN,**   the meaning of which you need to decipher on your own and prove to God that **you are the one worth being picked up.**

So, <u>**sharpen and focus your aware attention to get to the universal dimension**</u>. Don't accept the society-instilled stereotypes that so many people fall for, giving up on discovering their ***universally granted exceptionality,*** their unique personal essence for the material security and the "***Whatever!*** "choices in life .False goals frustrate, irritate, and end up in a wasted life. It's not stress that kills our lives, it's ***the betrayal of our goals*** that generates stress and allows the broken spirit to poison and disconnect our minds and hearts .

(Rule # 28 of Self-Renaissance)

Authenticate Your Unique Fate!

God-Given *Exceptionality* is Always Without Any Banality!

A great Catalonian architect- **Antonio Gaudi** *- The House of Gauley - Barcelona*

Universally Authenticate Your Unique Fate!

5. The Luminosity of the Vintage You

If you are consciously working on transforming yourself into **the Ultimate Best Vision of You**, or the **Vintage You** , the guidance of the universal dimension of life will always be with you, securing your exceptionality and supporting your faith in it. You will start appreciating yourself more and judging others less .Uplift your mood with the main auto-induction to boost your spirit and keep on realizing your exceptionality against any odds by learning and doing more.

I Can…! I want to…!And I will…!

Have you ever noticed how luminous some people are? Sometimes, I meet a black person and get totally carried away by his / her inner light. This interior illumination outshines the skin color, racial differences, education, position, and any social prejudices. I met many people like that in the USA. .**Inner grace is always streaming forth with faith!**

As I have repeatedly indicated above, when I say, *faith,* I do not mean dogmatic *religious piousness* when a person talks about redemption but is devoid of inner light and is full of depression and anger. I mean faith in its true, enlightening **body + spirit + mind** unity when a person's words and actions are in synch with the God's wink! To manage your life in time and space, you need to have a lot of self-inducted grace!

I know who I am!

I am a strong, calm, bold, and determined owner of my firm will!

I can *become more conscious,* **I want to** *be more conscious,* **I will!** *become more conscious! **I am becoming more and more compassionate / kind/ considerate/ honest faithful** etc.* with each coming day!

I'm My Best Friend; I'm My Beginning and My End!

6. Self-Consciousness Formation is in the Self-Education and Fractal Unification!

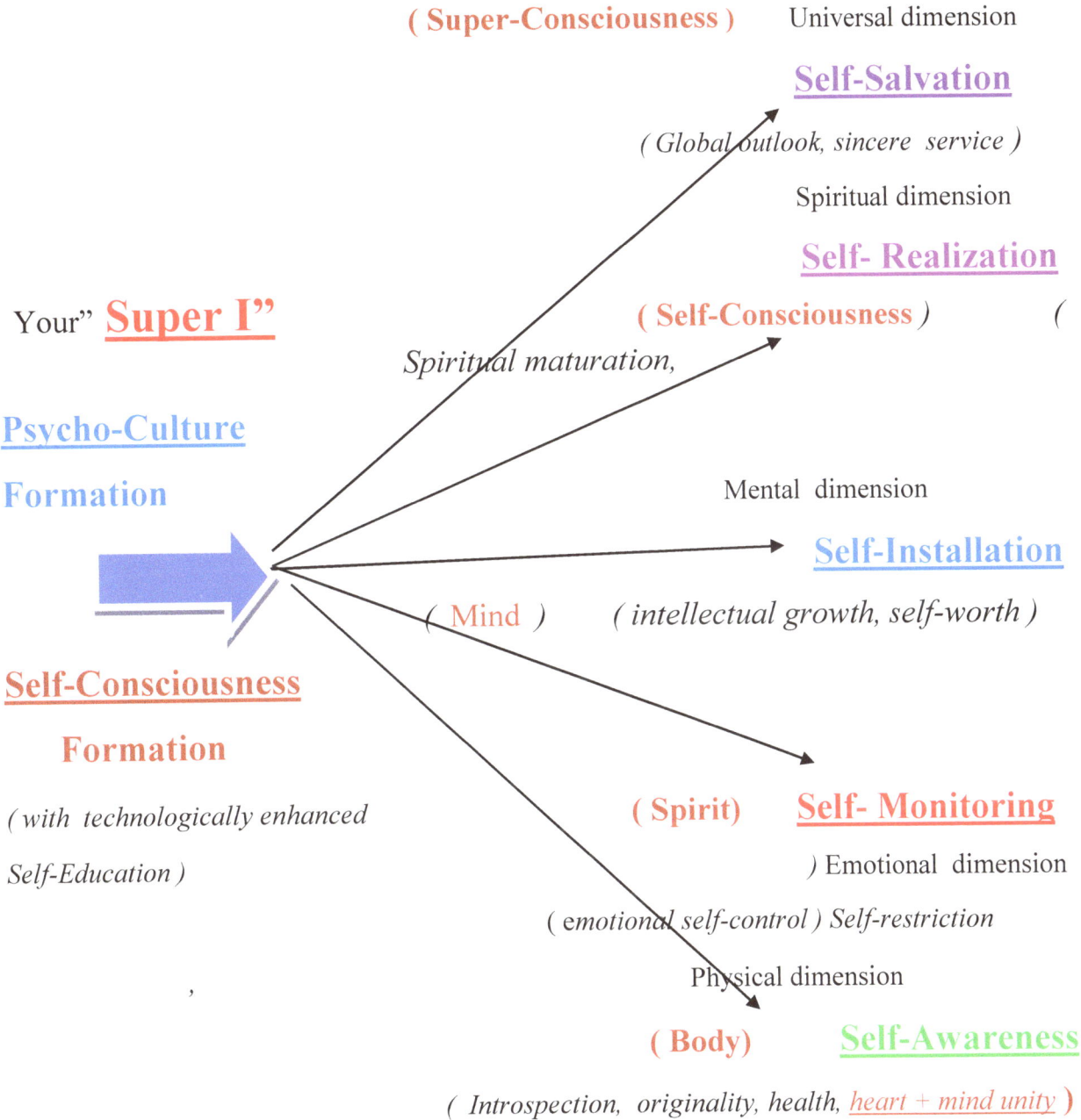

(Super-Consciousness) Universal dimension

Self-Salvation

(Global outlook, sincere service)

Spiritual dimension

Self- Realization

Your" **Super I"**

(Self-Consciousness) (

Spiritual maturation,

Psycho-Culture

Formation

Mental dimension

Self-Installation

(Mind) *(intellectual growth, self-worth)*

Self-Consciousness

Formation

(with technologically enhanced

Self-Education)

(Spirit) **Self- Monitoring**

) Emotional dimension

(emotional self-control) Self-restriction

Physical dimension

,

(Body) **Self-Awareness**

(Introspection, originality, health, heart + mind unity)

Body + Spirit + Mind + Self- Consciousness+ Super-Consciousness

= A Whole, Intellectualized Spiritually Self!

Self-Worth is the Inner Integrity Force!

7. Mind-to-Mind + Heart-to-Heart Evolution

Science proves that most of our thinking is done in the perception area. Perception is how we look at things., and how aware of life we are. Meanwhile, our students hardly know anything about the brain. Their **LIVING INTELLIGENCE** must be enriched with the new insights from neuroscience about the flexibility of the brain and its plasticity, on the one hand, and **the heart + mind communication,** on the other. *"The genetic fusion of the heart cells and the cells of the mind is a different way of embracing our potential." (Gregg Brandon*)

It's an amazing ability of the **NEUROLOGICAL UNITY** of the heart and the brain to adjust to the reality and empower us with the Emotional Diplomacy in it. The development of this electro-magnetic **innate unity** should be the main goal of our technologically baked education. Science, for instance, can alter the synaptic connections in the brain and change the language behavior patterns

A regular human interaction in the **mind-to-mind,** not **heart-to-heart** communication. must be changed to **mind + heart** unity. Such symbiosis will make the interaction even with a machine more meaningful in the virtual reality. So, learn to see the exceptionality in your kids and life partners. No sarcasm and criticism.

Also, being right does not mean necessarily that we immediately must find someone who is wrong. *"The finger pointing to the moon is not the moon".(Buddha)* One of the reasons we often must deal with ignorance at work lies in the fact that ignorant people lack intelligence due to their *patterned thinking blindness* that is never challenged. It must be destroyed with a new flood of consciously processed **professional awareness** that. new times sweep ignorance with.

The Neurological Understanding of the Brain Affects Our Life's Gain!

8. Self-Gravity Formation is Our Main Technologically Channeled Obligation!

I keep accentuating in every book that the Universal level of self-creation is *the determining one in our life's mission* because our God-given exceptionality is driving us through life.

Exceptionality is your Personal Gravity!

Your exceptionality is the starting visual point for the mind's extra---terrestrial flights into the impossible. Your imaginary plan might seem to be lame to someone, but you must stand by it with determination!

The idea that defies the common - flies ; the one that is restricted by it - dies!

Your exceptionality with its magnetic power *should be grounded in your soul* before it is launched into the public space. Your universal mission will be guiding you and literally supporting your spirit to be infinite!

Being goal- wired, we become self-inspired!

Being guided by the Universal Intelligence also means your constant work on Self-Renaissance! The fractal unity of your holistic self-creation might get broken unless you establish a firm connection between the heart and the mind and finally tune to your INTUITION. This connection embraces the relationship with your loved ones and the people that pass through your life . Only *putting the heart and the mind in sync* can we get the God's wink of approval, or can we synchronize ourselves with the vibrations of the Universal Mind that is emitting them non-stop and that the genius of *Nicola Tesla* was teaching us to perceive "*as free energy transmitted to us.*"

(Body + Spirit + Mind) + (Self-Consciousness + Universal Consciousness)

9. Great Minds Don't Have a Superiority Complex!

In sum, the formation of self-gravity, that I have defined above will enable you to apply your *Emotional Diplomacy Skills* to the holistic self-transformation that will **INEVITABLY** illuminate your personality with **CHARISMA** which is, in fact, the ability to put your *Heart + Mind* sync on the front seat of Your Emotional Diplomacy Link!

<u>**Make Your heart Smart and the Mind kind. Be One of a Kind!**</u>

The gravity of the heart+ mind unity gives us might, but it must be earned in the fight! I do not mean any confrontation here, I mean the willpower and determination, enlightened with the assuredness that you are right in your exceptional vision of your goal in life. Being right also means acting with aware attention and applying proactive purposeful thinking. So, self-renaissance demands not only **a mind-to-mind interaction,** but also *a* **heart-to-heart connection!**

As a matter of fact, we need to generate **SELF-GRAVITY** in every aspect of our life, starting with the very top of the society - the government, its divisions, parties, groups, banks, businesses, and our families.

Every aspect of our being demands *physical, emotional, professional, financial, spiritual, and universal gravity* not just de juror, but the facto. In other words, being exceptional means to be holistically extra-ordinary in every stratum of life. *Make your exceptionality your Godly fort and the prayer everywhere.* People gravitate to the top dogs that are seemingly accomplished people, but very often they <u>have not developed their own personal gravity</u> *physically. emotionally, mentally, spiritually, and universally.*

Education is Not just Learning; It's Also Self-Gravity Forming!

Section 2

(Self-Salvation Stage of a Self-Renaissance Sage)

Self-Worth

is a

Self-Gravity

Force!

Self-Gravity ability is developed by Self-Suggestibility!

(Rule # 29 of Self-Renaissance)

Nothing is Impossible if You Make Your Self-Creation Irreversible!

1. Self-Renaissance is a Universal Dance!

To stay on the path of ***realizing your exceptionality***, you need to <u>unplug your energy cord from the society's stereotyped outlet</u> that is energized by the mass media destructive mess.

You should consciously plug it into **the mind + heart** outlet of your own rising **SELF-CONSCIOUSNESS** that is inseparable from Super-Consciousness, or the Universal Intelligence that we all perceive as God. **Individuality and authenticity** are the essential qualities on the path of Self-Renaissance. **Being sincere beats dishonesty and fear!**

The main question for us now is* HOW *to build up our communication with* <u>the Universal Electro-Magnetic Field</u> *and do it consciously.

So, to attain more mental-emotional control and establish order in life, every time that your spirit goes down, immediately fill up your willpower tank with the auto-suggestive gas, or the ***essential self-induction.*** You will boost the sense of exceptionality in you.

<u>**I am a strong, bold, calm, and determined owner of my firm will!**</u>

I can   *take charge of my thoughts, words, feelings ,and action.*

I want to   *take charge of my thoughts, words, feelings ,and action,*

And I will *take charge of my thoughts, words, feelings ,and action*

I am becoming better and better at……with each coming day!

<u>**I'm in love with myself. I keep surpassing myself!**</u>

(For more on self-monitoring, see the book " I'm Free to Be the Best of Me!"-2020")

(Rule # 29 of Self- Renaissance)

My Self-Salvation is in the Inner Spiritual Maturation!

2. The Universal Music of Life!

I am in a music hall

Of the universal vastness of All!

What I hear inside

Is the music of Life!

The symphony of the ocean

Is like Chopin's finales in motion.

I admire the diction

Of every chord's friction!

It fills me up with awe,

And with so much more!

We need to get in touch

With the music of life, so much!

Only in the seasons of its composition

Can we discover our personal mission!

Only in the harmony with its frequencies

Can we burry our human differences!

Only with Crescendo in the Heart and
Pianissimo in the Mind can We All
Survive as a Kind!

3. *"Religiousness is Following the Messenger; Spirituality is Following the Message"* (Sadhguru)

In my book *"Self-Taming"* *(spiritual level),* I write about the first computer image of **Jesus Christ** taken from **the Turin Shroud** and published on the cover of the "*Scientific American*" magazine in 1995.

It surprised me with its authenticity, and I made the copy of Christ's picture, framed it, and placed it over my writing table. ***Thus, the piercing eyes of Jesus Christ*** have become the main point of reference in my life. I came from the socialist atheistic world, but I have always had inner sacredness that connects us all to the Universal Intelligence / Consciousness that we perceive as God.

God is One with you and me; God is All we can feel and see!

So, I suggest you have the image of your spiritual guide in the mind as the reference point of goodness in you, reminding you to follow his messages. Also, get into the habit of inwardly **X-RAYING** yourself or conducting an integral **SELF-REFLECTION** in all five levels, starting from the Above. Scan your noble self-growth in the *universal, spiritual, mental emotional, and physical* terms every evening, before falling asleep and see how you progress in your self-growth.

First and foremost, assess your improvement on the path of the ***realization of your exceptionality,*** and judge your life by being consistent and faithful to your unique goal in life in every dimension.

We are all part of the Universal Intelligence, the Energy-Informational Field of Consciousness with its own plan of action for each life. You are here to realize it by proving your exceptionality that you must discover as the goal of your life at the universal level of your life.

Your Exceptionality is Charged by the Universal Mentality!

4. Turn Unconquerable Vulnerability into the Emotional Diplomacy Ability!

"The hardest work on Earth is to change yourself." (*Dalai Lama)* The weakness that is the hardest to overcome is the national, religious, and personal vulnerably that is the softest spot in our psyche - *our unconquered Ego.* Our untrained emotional make up is vulnerable to the unverified lies, critical observations of our mis-interpreted actions, one-sided judgement, and the inability to hear out the other partner.

Most traumatizing is a person's malicious, non-forgiving avalanche of accusations that are often forgotten in detail by another party. The misinterpretation of the past events *triggers the tsunami of emotions* in a   person who tries to rehabilitate himself. Such situations are often generated by women that are more emotional than men, and therefore, their *level of vulnerability management is* much lower, especially in love-hate dichotomy of feelings, occurring due to lack of personal gravity, when the heart and mind are in disconnection..

Body + Spirit + Mind + Self-Consciousness + Universal Consciousness

The body gets affected by stress, the spirit is broken, the mind is in a turmoil, the self-consciousness is very low, and the disconnection with the Universal Intelligence is absolute. Only *immediate awareness of this state of self-ecology* can help the one who got into that pit.

Self-Awareness will stop the process of the destructive emotional accumulation, and it will ground it then and there! The main self-induction" I know who I am! is lifesaving here. It helps you employ two powerful self-gravity weapons - silence and a smile. A smile is the tool to solve the problems, while silence helps not generate them.

Keep Working on the Gravity of Your Self-Exceptionality!

5. The Main Auto-Suggestive Meditation to Create Self-Gravity Elation.

Below, to be consistent, I will walk you again through a very simple, but most effective **Active Auto-Suggestive Meditation** It is very creative because autosuggestibility implies your own creative approach to the process of inducting yourself with the gravitational force of being your own boss.

Self-gravity brings back our mental-emotional sanity!

You know that active meditation involves consistent self-focus and the ability <u>to zero in on your own mental-emotional state</u>. It will also enhance your willpower considerably as any conscious action does. Auto-Suggestive meditation is also the best way to heighten your self-consciousness! In any problematic situation remind yourself of the mind-set: <u>I know who I am!</u>

I am a strong, calm, bold, and determined owner of my firm will!

I can...; I want to...; and I will...!

Learn to mentally induct yourself with whatever outcome you need by just **breathing in** slowly through the nose the first part of this. <u>Make a short pause</u>, instilling the formula in your core. **Breathe out** slowly through the mouth the second part of it.

<u>These are the most basic inductive actions.</u> Appreciate the joint work of your mind and heart in sync. To feel the heart, put the thumb of your right hand on the pulse point on the wrist of your left hand. Listen to its beat: *21-21-21...* Your mind and heart get in sync. *You feel but think!*

(Rule # 30 of Self- Renaissance)

Put a Smile on Your Face! Let Your Personality Surface!

6. There is no Self-Renaissance without the Emotional Diplomacy Maintenance!

In every book on Self-Resurrection *(See Book Rationale),* I ask you to use the self-boosting mind-set to stabilize yourself. - **I'm my best friend; I'm my beginning and my end!** Use it as often as you need the support for your self-esteem in action-taking, Also, try to upload any autosuggestion , resonating with you while reading this book. Note it, please; you need to do the Suggestive Meditation *in synch with breathing,* underline connecting your heart and the mind. Induct yourself with any ending to the formula that you need to enhance your health, love, enthusiasm, etc. Use, for instance,

I can be healthy, I want to be healthy, and I will be healthy.

Breathe in the first two words of the mind-set. *Hold the breath* for a few seconds, focusing your aware attention on the heart. Hear its rhythmic beat-21-21-21. Start *slowly breathing out* through the mouth, saying inwardly the auto-induction:

"I am becoming healthier and healthier, stronger and stronger, etc. with each coming day!"

Do it three times. Finish the active meditation with any self-induction of your choice. *My whines and tears, worries and fears* (breathe in) /- Pause - *varnish as the useless emotional garnish!* (breathe out).

Don't grudge your gladness, don't boast about your smartness, don't exaggerate your happiness, and don't complain about your inner darkness. *"Be the thing in itself"(Hegel); Be true to Yourself!*

We are gradually opening up to the world of Authenticity, Insightfulness, Honesty, Self-Power, and Synchronicity!

7. Activate Your Spirit to Be Infinite!

T In sum, the state of the spirit in you is fundamental for your *physical, emotional, mental, spiritual, and universal health.* We all know the maximum: "A healthy spirit is in a healthy body" , and vice versa.

Activating the spirit, you actualize your life!

Every religion is based on raising in its followers a solid faith and a strong spirit that enables a believer to get out of the darkness of ignorance to the light of life. Spiritual self-salvation is at the top of my five-dimensional paradigm of Self-Resurrection, too.*(See above)*

Self-Salvation must be based on **the salvation from the inner slavery** to fear, bad habits ignorance, sickness, gluttony, a sinful sex behavior, hate, racial , religious and material limitedness, passivity, laziness, and **lack of Self-Worth.** All our deficiencies are always generated by the lack of love for life, oneself, and others. The wish to become free of the slavery of the spirit is **the skill of making a characterful effort to defeat yourself consciously.** To tolerate the slavery of the spirit means to agree to be a slave of life, not its re-former and a re-builder.

"Change needs much thought effort."(Dr .Joe Dispenza)

The best of us try to be in inspired and in spirit , like *Nickola Tesla, Steve Jobs, Bill Gates, Elon Musk, Jeff Bezos, Jack Ma, Mark Zuckerberg, Reid Hoffman, Ray Kurzweil* and many other leaders of the exponential innovations. They are changing the world by having changed themselves! Artificial intelligence, robotics, and the wonders of the Internet are being unleashed thanks to their exceptional minds. Being governed by their universal exceptionality, we get inspired to surpass ourselves in the NOW for our future WOW.!.

(Rule # 31 of Self- Renaissance)

Being the Best is a Tough Test!

8. Conclude the Journey in the Universal Dimension of Self-Resurrection!

The Reminder: Having completed **the Universal level** of reviewing *"Self-Renaissance"* essential standpoints, don't forget to conduct **SELF-SCANNING,** following the evolutionary paradigm

Self-Synthesis ➡ *Self-Analysis* ➡ *Self-Synthesis!*

(Self-Awareness) → *(Self-Monitoring + Self-Installation +Self-Realization)* → *(Self-Salvation)*

Self-Synthesis starts with making up the **HOLISTIC PICTURE OF SELF** every day , doing it most objectively ,consciously, and honestly.

Self-Analysis must be conducted as a quick review of your *physical, emotional, mental, spiritual, and universal* realms of life. This **SELF X-RAYING** will show you what strata of life you succeed or fail in.

Analyze 1) *your health* and the physical activity. **2)** *the attitude to yourself* and the people around you, **3)** *new knowledge* that you enriched your intelligence with and the strategic plan of action, leading to your full professional self-realization, 4) *your faith* and following its messages in action. **5)** *commitment to your exceptionality,* your goal in life. Don't ever betray your self-worth!

Final Self-Synthesis – Completing the **SELF-ASSESSMENT,** *give yourself grades for each level separately* and figure out the average grade for the day, on your own scale - *(3.5 /,4, 6 etc.)* In other words, you must assess the ability to manage yourself in the time and space of the changing reality. Your **"SUPER I"** must be constantly self-assessed!. Self-scanning, *as a general, objective vision of Self,* is very beneficial if you visualize the paradigm of self-creation, inducting yourself with,

My Human Essence is in Constant Spiritual Renaissance!

Our Protection from the Above is the Real Stuff!

(Best Photos, Internet Collection)

God's Brain is One, and We are One in It!

Stage Four

(Self-Monitored Stage of a Self-Renaissance Sage)

Spiritual Dimension - Self-Realization

Your Life Essence

is in

the Spiritual

Self-Renaissance

Use the present-day technology to maintain your

Self-Monitored Inner Ecology!

Self-Renaissance is the Faith-Relationship with Yourself!

God is Me; God is My Philosophy!

Self-Culture Means Holistically Based Self-Acculturation!

Self-Renaissance

Form   +   Content

(Body+ Spirit+ Mind) + (Self-Consciousness + Universal Consciousness)

Living Intelligence   +   Enlightened Self-Consciousness = A Whole Self!

- -

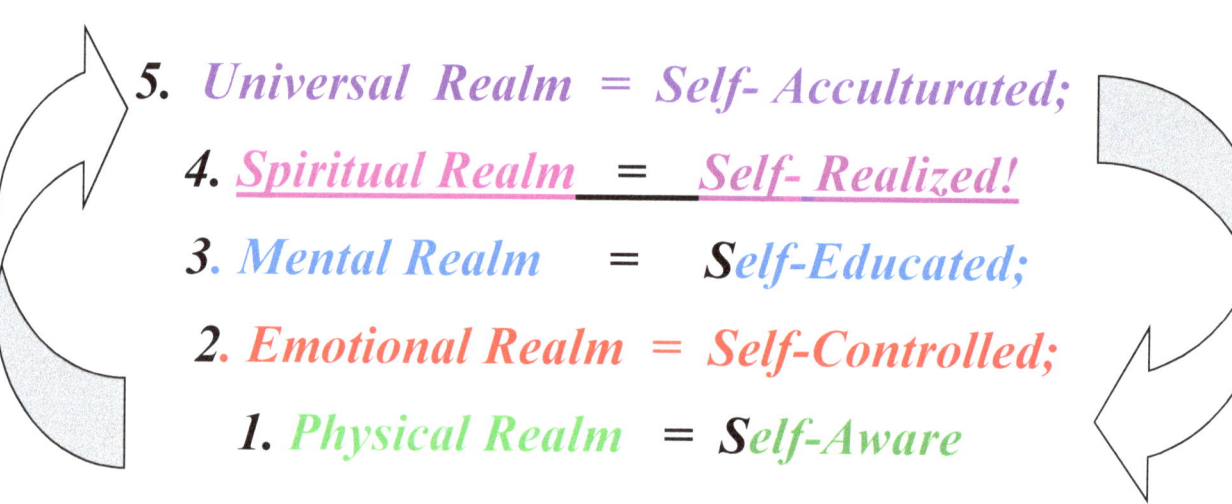

5. *Universal Realm = Self- Acculturated;*

4. *Spiritual Realm = Self- Realized!*

3. *Mental Realm   =   Self-Educated;*

2. *Emotional Realm = Self-Controlled;*

1. *Physical Realm = Self-Aware*

The Harmony of the Heart + Mind Sync is the Main Goal of the Emotional + Mental link = Personal Gravity = Raised Self-Consciousness

The process of raising Self-Consciousness is very complicated and must be consciously monitored by everyone of us, willing to upgrade their physical, emotional, mental, spiritual, and universal status in life.

The New Culture of Self-Acculturation is in

Self-Consciousness Formation.

Section 1

(Self-Realization Stage of a Self-Renaissance Sage)

A New, Godly and Holistically Developed Self!

The Resurrection of Crist *stands as the defining point in the history of the humanity. No other event before or since, has impacted society, culture, art, science, literature and civilization at large to such a degree.* <u>But have we become better?</u> *We still rely on the messages of the religious leaders that define our limited religious pluralism. Even at this most mesmerizing technological outburst, we turn to technology to help us with the messages that we ourselves are unable to interpret.* Time has come to prove to God that you are able to do what He thought! Tune your **AUTO-ANTENNA** to God; modify your thought!!

<u>Self-Renaissance is the proof of your Spiritual Commitment!</u>

(Rule # 32 of Self-Renaissance)

In My Thought, I Report Only to God!

1. Actionable Self-Creation

Life is the act of <u>**Godly creation**</u> for a person who is developing a **NEW SENSE OF IDENTITY,** the identity of a person with *"spiritualized intelligence"(Dr. Fred Bel), raised self-consciousness*, and the reestablished unity of the heart and. the mind that must always be driven by curiosity and hunger for new knowledge. *"The pursuit of truth and beauty is a sphere of activity in which we are permitted to remain children all our lives."* (Albert Einstein)

The route is to move from the subjective, religiously limited vision of life to ***the objective, scientifically grounded vision of Self*** and the life around as God's creation. The paradigm of such vision is based on a <u>**fractal formation**</u> and our godly holistic :transformation

<u>**Body + Spirit + Mind + Self- Consciousness+ Super-Consciousness.**</u>

There are many spiritually grounded mind-sets in this book. You may upload them into your mind with the help of your smart phone at any time. On the spiritual track of Self-Renaissance, we need to be constantly reminded of the God-given messages that <u>**make us people of the same values in any religion.**</u> It's paramount to instill these values in the heads of our kids. The Oneness of the godly sanity unites our hearts and minds and helps us hear each other without any vanity!

A godly person hardly ever loses his / her tempo, yells, or intentionally hurts religious or national feelings of another. But in the turmoil of the present-day reality, we disregard these values. So, everyone needs the Emotional Diplomacy Skills to be auto-suggestively instilled. We all address our prayers to God when the trouble hits , but we need to make our appeals to God unconditioned, love-based and conscious.

Long Live the Belief in God without IF!

2. The Interconnectedness and Unanimity Form Our Spiritual Gravity!

Unfortunately, for centuries, irrespective of our religiously blind faith, **we're moving outside the divinely programmed matrix** with limited and unconscious life's dynamics in our minds. We know it, but we are not aware of it because **we live automatically and soul-statically.** The super-genius of our time, **Nikola Tesla,** said, *"Everything that lives is related to a deep and wonderful relationship. – man, and the stars, amoebas, and the Sun, the heart, and the circulation of the infinite number of worlds. Their ties are unbreakable, but they can be tamed."*

That's why recognizing and respecting all the religions is a natural and holistic process of our evolution. **The initial role of religion in the growth of our spirituality is inarguable** and the recently unveiled and discovered digital essence of the Universe leaves no doubt of our connection to *the Master Computer* that we all perceive as God.

But true spirituality shouldn't be dogmatic in its **form + content** perception of God. Godliness in us ,or **the Laws**, *given by Moses +* **Grace,** c*oming from Christ or any other spiritual leader* **form the bases of our godliness and humanness.** But our religious manifestations in the form of crosses that we wear, the way we cut our hair, pray to different images, etc. should stop being a demonstration .It must become a true **faith + knowledge** driven elation - the elation of *Self-Resurrection!*

Religion and science must stop being in defiance!

I suggest you have the image of your spiritual leader in your inner vision, testing your feelings, words, and actions with his piercing eyes. *Evil's grip of ignorance gets loosened* where spiritualized intelligence embraces the mind and the heart with the new knowledge grip.

Life-Gaining is in Self-Taming!

3. Do Not Faith-Trifle; Read Torah, Koran, and the Bible!

Do not faith-trifle,

Read Torah, Koran, and the Bible!

Do it slowly and, consciously,

Seriously, and prayerfully!

These sacred books are the mines of wealth

And the rivers of our inner health!

They divinely soul-invest

Their holiness and life's zest!

Any sacred book, indeed,

Helps us out-power the evil seed!

We get into the paradise of glory

And receive the remedy against any soul's folly!

We start to apply less eloquence

And learn to use more patience and tolerance!

Then, the wisdom of the spiritual word

Becomes our shield and the unbreakable sword!

With the spiritual clarity,

Life loses its primitive vanity!

(Rule # 33 of Self-Renaissance)

So, Be Consistent with the Word of the Holy Books that You've Got!

4. In God's Account, We All Count!

Fractals of Self-Symmetry Generate Our Personal Gravity!

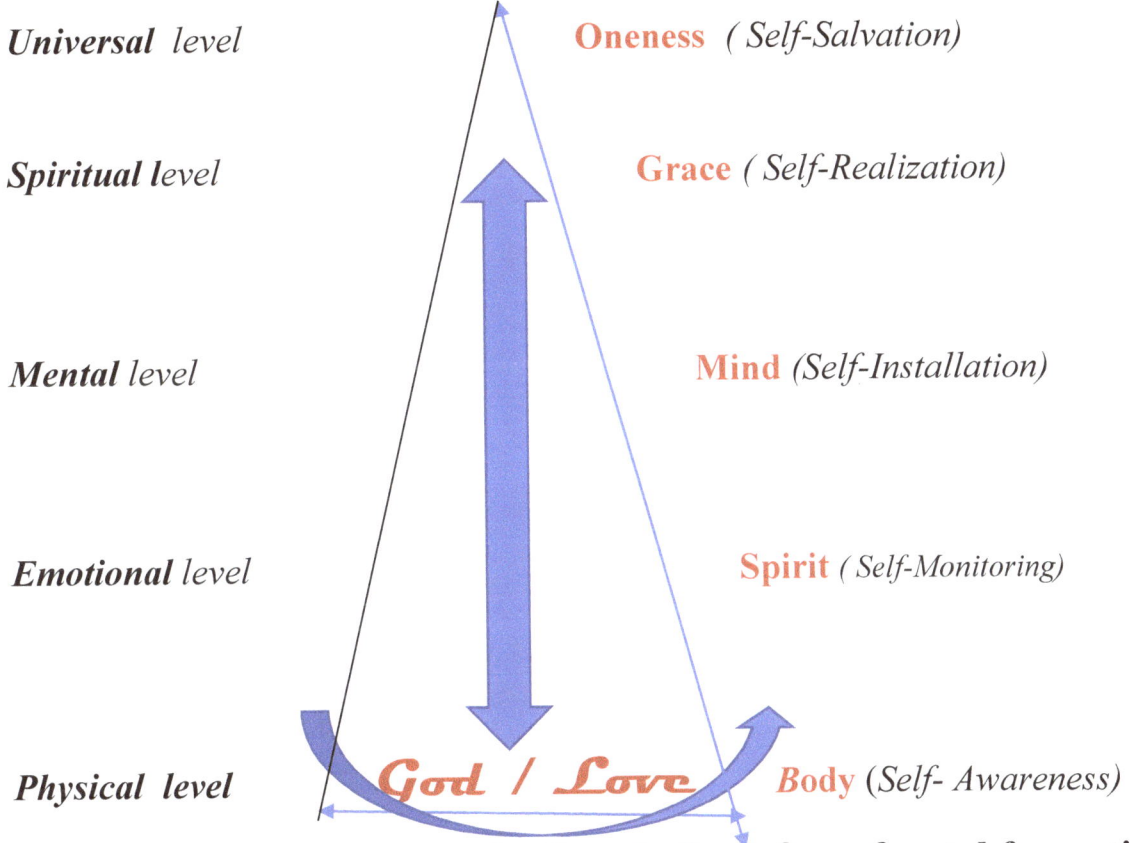

| Universal level | Oneness (Self-Salvation) |

| Spiritual level | Grace (Self-Realization) |

| Mental level | Mind (Self-Installation) |

| Emotional level | Spirit (Self-Monitoring) |

| Physical level | God / Love   Body (Self- Awareness) |

God and Love are at the foundation of our fractal formation!

BODY + SPIRIT + MIND + GRACE + ONENESS or

Body+ Spirit + Mind+ Self-Consciousness + Super- Consciousness

Thus, with the help of the Love from the Above, we are forming our spiritualized life fractals, the SOLAR SYSTEM of our families, the love relationships that we have, and our own inner self. That's why God is Love, and our *Emotional Diplomacy Gravity* must be based on love that has a wide eternal meaning..

Self-Sustained Love is the Gravity of Our Universal Unity!

Section 2

(Self-Realization Stage of a Self-Renaissance Sage)

Praying is
the Auto-Inductive
Soul-Framing!

Any religious foundation is people's formation!

God is not any religious wearing, "God is My Self-Bearing!"

(Fyodor Dostoevsky)

The Statemen:" **Christ died for our sins"** *sounds strange now because our sinfulness is increasing by the day.*

So, do not sway from the Self-Renaissance way! Seize the day!

"Born from flesh is flesh. born from spirit is spirit. All of you need to be born from Above." *(Sayings of Jesus Christ",1971)*

Every Burden is a Blessing! -Appreciate your family, kids, health, a job, the people around, the troubles in life - *You are alive!!!*

(Best Photos, Internet Collection)

(Rule # 34 of Self-Renaissance)

See Who You Pick into Your Solar System of Love!

1. The Prayer for Sanity and Emotional Gravity!

Teach me, God,
To have the sight,
Teach me to tell
The wrong from the right.

Teach me, Father,
To sing and to dance,
Teach me to appreciate
The life given chance!

Teach me to share
What I begot,
Teach me to dare
What I haven't got!

Teach me to live
In the Now,
To break the strains of the past
And get the future skills of "How?"

Teach me to love
The entire life,
Teach me to cherish
Every day and night!

Teach me to serve
On the mission of Love,
Teach me to receive
The grace from the Above!

(Rule # 35 of Self-Renaissance)

See Good in Everything to Become Very Good at Something!

2. The Spiritual Role in Realizing Your Exceptionality Goal!

We often feel cornered in life due to the loss of the goal that is always connected with **the realization of self-exceptionality**, granted to us from the Above. The rightly set goal in life leads to full self-realization that is possible if a person set his goal in life in accord with his inclination, a unique gift, his exceptionality, a yearning of his / her soul. Proving your uniqueness means always swimming against the current and living through the unpleasant moments of a caterpillar state. The best among us are those that are true to themselves and their goals!

In order to come to a butterfly state and become an evolved being, we need to have a qualitatively different **INNER CONTENT** of life, with sincere praying and meditating, putting the entire Self into this process of self-reformation with **God as the messenger and you as the Sculptor.** Like grass, finding its way through the concrete, you need to take off the society-conditioned outfit and become a free individual, able to breathe, think, and act in a new embryo state that, like a pregnant mother,. you must bring to birth.

Reject, resist, reform your shaky, weak, fearful uniform!

We grow from a physical unripe state to **the spiritual maturity** of the highest rate in constant resistance This message was the highest of Christ's teachings that directed us to the search of heaven in ourselves.

Then, being sincere and having a pure soul's voice, we can get connected to God in any place on Earth. **That's why God is Omnipresent,** and the authenticity of our connection with the Divine on the path of justifying the Universal trust is engraved in all of us

In Life's Trinity (Body + Spirit + Mind) is Our Universal Infinity!

3. To Forgive is the Hardest Job to Achieve!

Next, Self-Renaissance is impossible without forgiveness of the others' digressions These destructive feelings are in the way of your inner renaissance. .To be constantly "supervised" from the Above entails not only the chance of illuminating yourself, but also <u>the responsibility of illuminating others</u> with your inner grace, wisdom, and. balance.

Propel your awe of thought to be worthy of God!

Neither of us is perfect, and it's impossible to get on with our self-growth without forgiving oneself and others for the wrong done in the impulsive state of mind..

We apologize, but we don't become wise!

Forgiving is the feeling that is the hardest to accomplish because it is very hard to delete the memory of the pain from the <u>mind and the heart in sync.</u> *The mind reminds you of the pain though it's gone from the heart..* That's why we say, ***"I forgive, but I don't forget."***

The subconscious mind does not delete the file of an offence. You need ***to re-load your memory with the pleasant moments of dealing with this person.*** There are always good things to remember. That's why, Emotional Diplomacy means to see deeper into the one that failed you and said something painful in an emotional turmoil.

Be kind to the unkind. Be One of a kind!

.Make a great gesture, forgive your offender then and there! Do not make him / her apologize again. ***The first attempt for an apology is sincere, the next one is forced.*** Betrayals, though, of a ***"stab in the back"*** malicious kind with an intention to take advantage of the situation for oneself, should never be forgiven. He / she doesn't qualify for any space and time in YOUR SOLAR SYSTEM'S TWINE! *Leo Tolstoy wrote,*

"A betrayal feels like your arms are cut - the pain's gone, but you cannot embrace with them."

4. "Reject, Resist, and Reform" Your Imperfect Inner Uniform!

Shake off the burden of hurt and damage from your cells with your monitored Alternate Breathing that you can always supplement with the *Auto-Suggestive meditation*. **Breathe in** (*through the left nostril ;the right is closed*)—SO – *pause and focus your aware attention on the heart*--H-A-A-M-M-M.(*breathe out slowly through the right nostril, closing the left one.*) *Do it in the opposite direction Also, do the Alternate Breathing with the words* **Calm down.**

Technology will help us record the moment of discord so you could see it later together. Visual proof helps both parties feel relieved because you don't perform any surgical operations" *who said and did what*". It's there. No clarifications and justifications , please; you'll fall into the confrontation pit again! There is another aspect to forgiveness , and it relates to the urge to strike back, to hurt the offender, to have a revenge on him / her. A great statement of Christ about the second cheek being displayed for a fist of an offender in such situation is inarguable because you must not belittle yourself to the offender's level. We know it, but we are not aware of it, nor do we follow it.

However, such response needs *Emotional Diplomacy* to be displayed de facto, not de juror. As a matter of fact, we need to thank the people that have harmed us for making us stronger, more able to reject, resist, and reform our imperfect inner uniform. Indeed, our enemies make us unbeatable in protecting our exceptionality, our goals, and our faith in our self-realization against any odds. Don't get involved into their evil race, be unshakable in your *knowledge – grounded, sincere faith!*

(Rule # 36 of Self-Renaissance)

Forgiveness is Me; Forgiveness is My Philosophy!

5. Calling on God to Help the Godly and the Godless.

Dear God! Bless the godly

And the godless!

Bless all those, that look ahead

With hopes in the outlet!

Bless the ones who commit crime and theft,

Bless those that are luck bereft.

Bless the rich to share

Bless those who lost faith to beware!

Bless us all

And let us never forget

About the Power of Life

And You in it!

Be Kind to the Unkind. I'm One of a Kind!

Make your Heart Smart and the Mind Kind! Be One of a Kind!

(Rule # 37 of Self-Renaissance)

If You Want to Spiritually Reboot,

Be in a Hurry to Do Something Good!

6. Everyday Self-Renaissance Provision

Perform your mission on the planet Earth to define your exceptional self-worth!

<u>I know who I Am!</u>

My Self-Renaissance is on the Go;

I'm in the Self-Resurrection Flow!

I am a strong, bold, calm, and determined owner of my firm will!

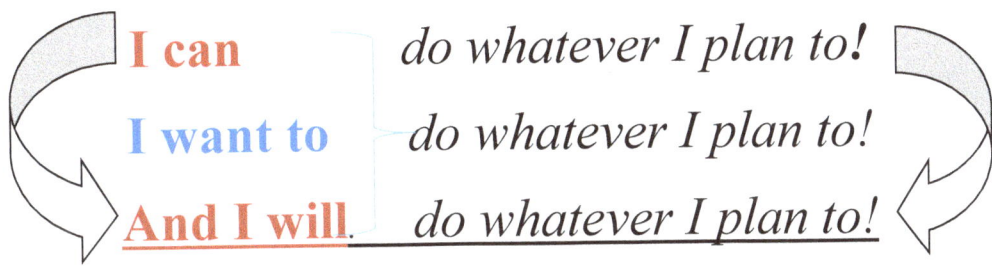

I can   *do whatever I plan to!*

I want to   *do whatever I plan to!*

And I will.   *do whatever I plan to!*

I am becoming better and better at……with each coming day!

<u>*Without forgiveness , there is no High Wisdom's reactiveness!*</u>

Once you have consciously based your life on **grace, sincerity, kindness, compassion, dignity, and love of life***, you will never get down the rocky road of self-corrode again.. The sacred messages of your spiritual leaders that are sowed in you for life will protect you from any selfish strife.((See the book "Self- Taming" for more .www.language-fitness.com)*

(Rule # 38 of Self-Renaissance)

So, Never Lose the Sight of Your <u>Divine Might!</u>

Spirit is Me; Spirit is My Philosophy!

(A great Russian artist - Isaac Levitan)

If the Sun disappeared in a Cloudy Mass,

It's a Chance for You to Get Calm and Relax.

It's There. It's in the Blue!

It's Everywhere; It's in You!

7. The Heaven and Hell are Inside Yourself!

(A Spiritual Message)

Creativity is heaven; destruction is hell,

We all know that very well!

But just to know it is not enough,

We also need to be better aware of that!

Heaven is our cognitive creativity,

While hell is a self-destructive infinity!

We need to stop talking with negation

And start living with a positive elation!

"It takes only a stroke to change a minus into a plus"

And be self-constructive, thus!

Your thinking transforms

And it stops accepting the negative forms.

You gradually realize that the hell

Is hidden in your emotional cell!

Since God is ruling the world, and that is true,

He's in charge of the hell inside of you, too!

Your new perception of the God's world

Will teach you to see the self-created under-world.

So, thanking God for the life's heaven and hell,

We immediately remove the evil spell!

If the lesson is learned,

The balance of life is restored!

Thus, the heaven and heling

Are only in our polarity dwelling!

If we remove polarity from our divided minds,

Life will get into the universal twines.

We'll be able to resist

The evil spirits' twists!

The music of life will fill us up with elation

And a true life-loving inspiration!

Then the Temple of SOLOMON

Will get built in our inner unified form!

Remember, we are responsible for the state of self-consciousness in our kids. It's vital for their self-creation to preserve the climate of mutual respect, joy, contentment, and happiness at home. *Their soul-maintenance and self-renaissance are your responsibility!* To establish the climate of synergy at home, we need to be sincere with ourselves and our kids.

Being honest deserves a love bonus! The authenticity of our thoughts, words, feelings and actions is tested by kids with the help of the technology. Kids trust their gadgets more than their parents now, and *our responsibility is to return their trust without an angry emotional gust.*

(Rule # 39 of Self-Renaissance)

The Multi-Dimensional Home Synergy Creates the Self-Renaissance Energy!

8. Conclude the Journey in the Spiritual Dimension with Self-Elation!

The Reminder: Having completed **the Spiritual level** of reviewing the essential standpoints of *Self-Renaissance,* don't forget to conduct **SELF-SCANNING,** following the evolutionary paradigm

Self-Synthesis ➡ **Self-Analysis** ➡ *Self-Synthesis!*

(Self-Awareness) ➡ *(Self-Monitoring + Self-Installation +Self-Realization)* ➡ *(Self-Salvation)*

Self-Synthesis starts with making up the **HOLISTIC PICTURE OF SELF** every day, *doing it most objectively, consciously, and honestly.*

Self-Analysis must be conducted as a quick review of your *physical, emotional, mental, spiritual, and universal* realms of life. This **SELF X-RAYING** will show you what circle of life you succeed in or fail .**Analyze** 1) *your health* and the physical activity**. 2)** *the attitude to yourself* and the people around you, **3)** *new knowledge* that you enriched your intelligence with and the strategic plan of action, leading to your full professional self-realization, 4) *your faith* and following its messages in action**.** *5) commitment to your exceptionality.*

Final Self-Synthesis – Completing the **SELF-ASSESSMENT,** *give yourself grades for each level separately* and figure out the average grade for the day, on your own scale - *(3.5 /,4, 6 etc.)* In other words, you must assess the ability to manage yourself in the time and space of the changing reality. Your "SUPER I" must be constantly self-assessed! Self-scanning, as a general, objective vision of Self, is very beneficial if you visualize the paradigm of self-creation. *It's like looking at the mirror of your soul,* inducting yourself with a justifiable mind-set,

(Rule # 40 of Self-Renaissance)

In My Life Quest, I'm the Best!

Stage Three

(Self-Installation Stage of a Self-Renaissance Sage)

Mental Dimension – Self-Installation

Self-Renaissance

and the Mental

Self-Management

" **The more intelligence a person is, the less important is his nationality!** "*(Ludmila Ulitskaya)*

(Rule # 41 of Self-Renaissance)

Holistically Knowledge-Steer; Your Mind is Life and Your Career!

Life's Oasis is Built on the Mental Basis!

(Best Photos- Internet Collection)

Unwind the Architecture of Your Mind!

Self-Culture Means Holistically Based Self-Acculturation!

Self-Renaissance

Form   +   Content

(Body+ Spirit+ Mind) + (Self-Consciousness + Universal Consciousness)

Living Intelligence   +   Enlightened Self-Consciousness = A Whole Self!

----

5. *Universal Realm = Self- Acculturated;*

4. *Spiritual Realm = Self- Realized!*

3. *Mental Realm = Self-Educated;*

2. *Emotional Realm = Self-Controlled;*

1. *Physical Realm = Self-Aware*

The Harmony of the Heart + Mind Sync is the Main Goal of the Emotional + Mental link = Personal Gravity = Self-Consciousness

consciously monitored by everyone of us, willing to upgrade their physical, emotional, mental, spiritual, and universal status in life.

The New Culture of Self-Acculturation is in

Self-Consciousness Formation.

Section 1

(Self-Installation Stage of a Self-Renaissance Sage)

Self-Renaissance Must be Educational!

"New Times are the times of Exponential Learning!"

(Ray Kurzweil)

Disconnection of Knowledge is the Death of Self-Power." *(Schopenhauer)*

1. Ten Vistas of Intelligence Must Support Our Self-Renaissance Diligence.

Our time is the **AGE OF TECHNOLOGICAL RENAISSANCE.** Our inner renaissance is generated by the vibratory frequencies of our rising self-consciousness that is boosted by our exponentially changing technological awareness. **AWARE ATTENTION** deletes frustration!

"**The power of the intellect is the magic of the mind!**"(*Byron , "Corsair")*

By raising self-consciousness in five philosophical levels – **mini, meta, mezzo, macro, and super**, or correspondingly, in five realms - *physical, emotional, mental, spiritual, and universal,* we create an integrated system of Self-Education, too. *A person's fractal self-growth must be based on ten essential levels of holistic. intelligence .*

(Body + Spirit + Mind) + (Self-Consciousness + Universal Consciousness)

The Vistas of Intelligence to mount on the path of Self-Renaissance are:

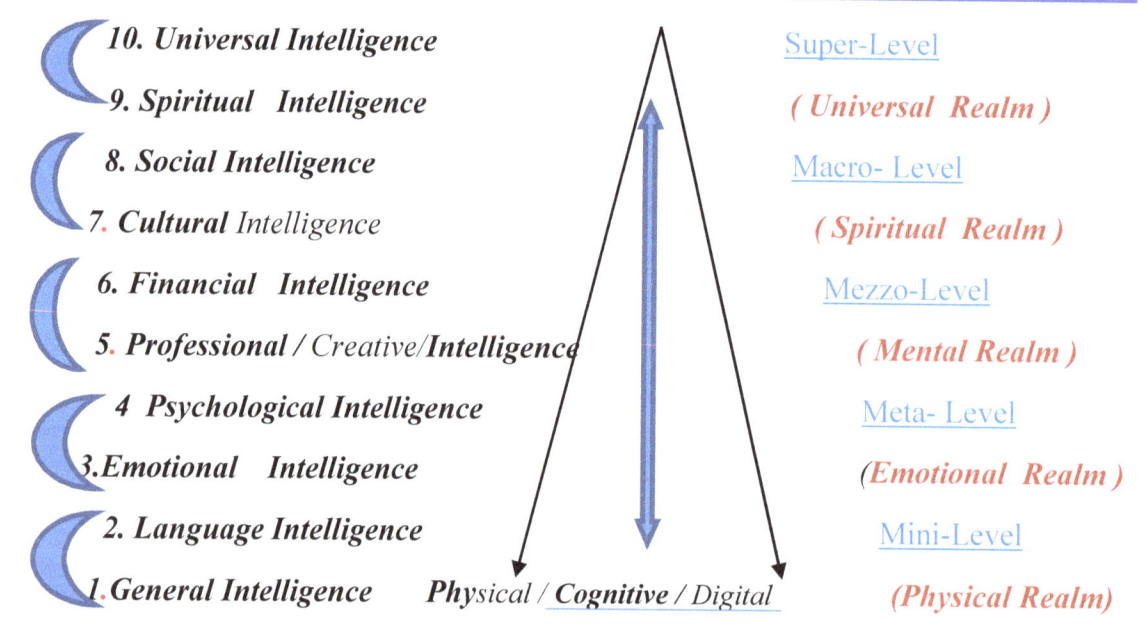

10. *Universal Intelligence*	Super-Level
9. *Spiritual Intelligence*	*(Universal Realm)*
8. *Social Intelligence*	Macro- Level
7. *Cultural* Intelligence	*(Spiritual Realm)*
6. *Financial Intelligence*	Mezzo-Level
5. *Professional / Creative/Intelligence*	*(Mental Realm)*
4 *Psychological Intelligence*	Meta- Level
3. *Emotional Intelligence*	*(Emotional Realm)*
2. *Language Intelligence*	Mini-Level
1. *General Intelligence* *Physical / Cognitive / Digital*	*(Physical Realm)*

*(See the Excellence Book Award winner" **Living Intelligence or the Art of Becoming!" /2020***

The More You Know; the Lighter Your Life's Burden Becomes!

2. Intelligence Refining is Life-Defining!

No doubt, a goal-oriented **self-refinement or Self-Renaissance** can be more productive if this process is monitored by the blueprint of the intellectual growth in <u>**five dimensions and ten levels of intelligence**</u> correspondingly. *(See the scheme below)* The holistic development of intelligence along these lines will inevitably raise your life-awareness and self-consciousness, expanding your intelligence in sync with the demands of the technological expansion. Such **INTEGRAL** *intellectual self-creation* will make your self-perfection more conscious, effective, and accurate. The vistas of intelligence are supposed to be acquired by the paradigm of <u>**Synthesis – Analysis – Synthesis,**</u> **too,** with alert awareness and **a conscious plan of action** according to which you can bridge the gaps in your general intelligence .knowingly .

<u>**The Ladder of the Intellectual Self-Renaissance**</u>

<u>**Synthesis**</u> *(Stages 1,2)* -<u>**Analysis**</u> *(Stages 3,4,5,6.7.8.)* -<u>**Synthesis**</u> *(Stages 9,10)*

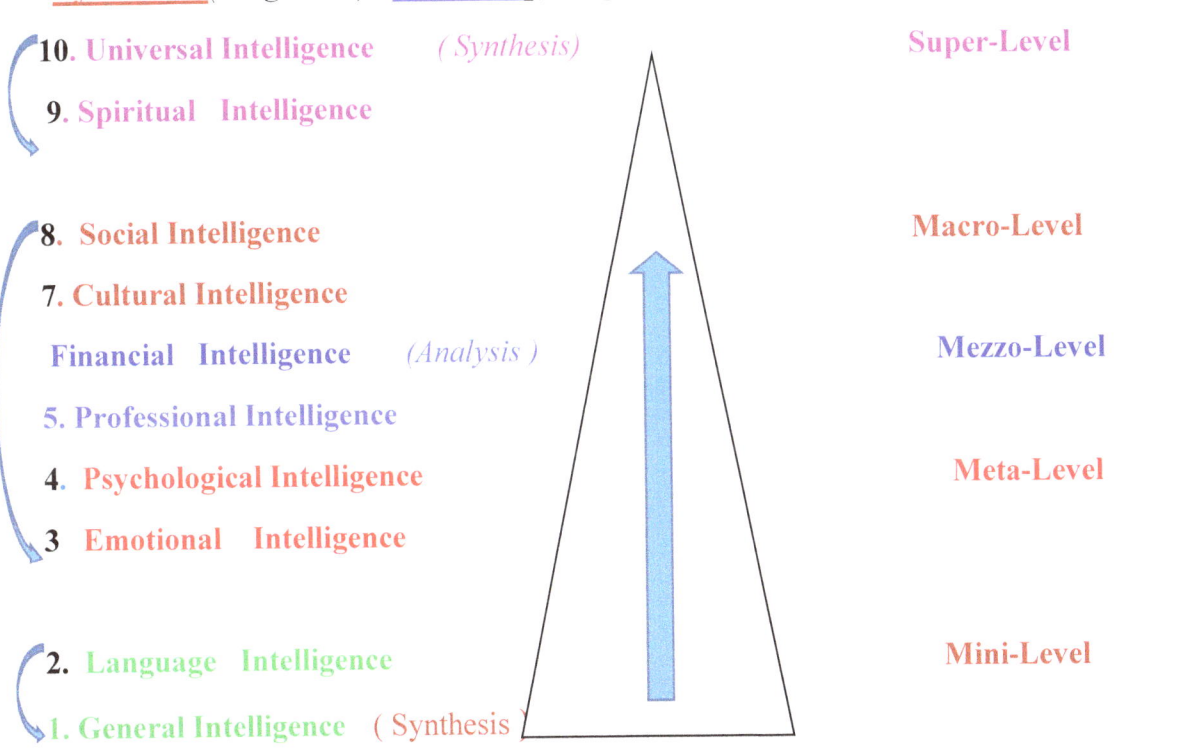

10. Universal Intelligence   *(Synthesis)*   **Super-Level**

9. Spiritual Intelligence

8. Social Intelligence   **Macro-Level**

7. Cultural Intelligence

Financial Intelligence   *(Analysis)*   **Mezzo-Level**

5. Professional Intelligence

4. Psychological Intelligence   **Meta-Level**

3 Emotional Intelligence

2. Language Intelligence   **Mini-Level**

1. General Intelligence (Synthesis)

We are all Life-Long Learners of the Art of Living!

3. The Ladder of Personal Gravity

Focusing on the Universal Intelligence, you must be modelling your life with a clear awareness of the levels of intelligence that you need to master to *be physically, emotionally, mentally, spiritually, and universally aristocratic.* <u>Self-Installation is in Self-Education!</u> ***"If I have seen further than other people, it's by standing upon the shoulders of giants."*** *(Albert Einstein)*

You want to base your mental Self-Management on your self-discovered **EXCEPTIONALITY-** an exceptional ability to do something better than others; the inner urge to make the world better by realizing your unique gift holistically , putting the <u>form + content</u> of your life in sync ***"Income never exceeds personal growth!"****(Reid Hoffman)*

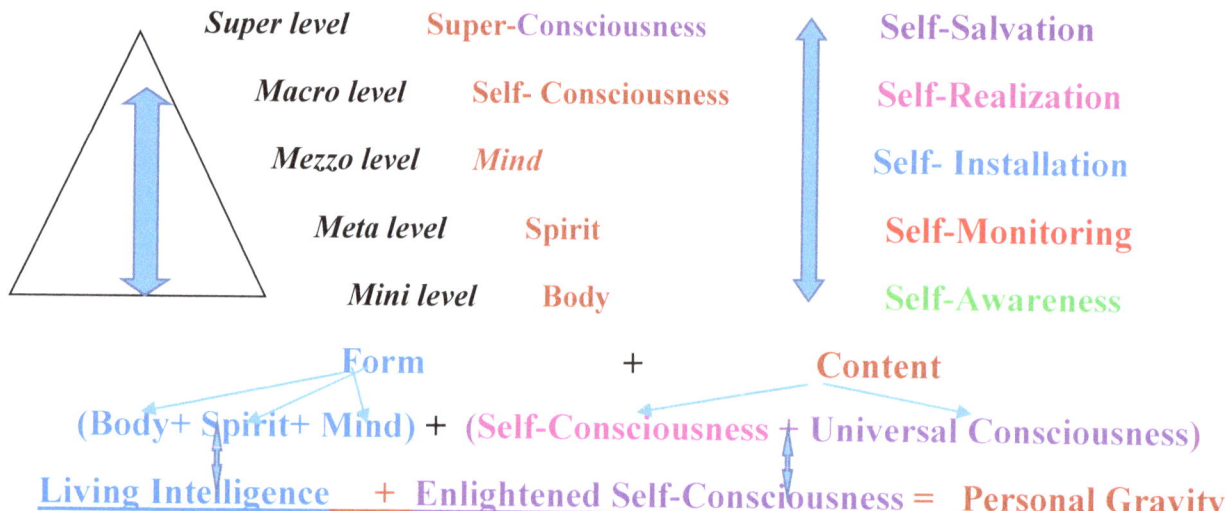

Super level	**Super-Consciousness**	**Self-Salvation**
Macro level	**Self- Consciousness**	**Self-Realization**
Mezzo level	*Mind*	**Self- Installation**
Meta level	**Spirit**	**Self-Monitoring**
Mini level	**Body**	**Self-Awareness**

Form + **Content**

(Body+ Spirit+ Mind) + **(Self-Consciousness + Universal Consciousness)**

<u>**Living Intelligence**</u> + **Enlightened Self-Consciousness** = **Personal Gravity!**

I have indicated in every book, featuring the mental level of self-growth how important it is to develop the **HOLISTIC THINKING SKILLS.** Holistic thinking will help us create the <u>**STERIO THINKING ABILITY**</u> that the digital expansion of thought **(left + right brains in sync)** demands from us now.

Mental Sanity + Emotional Diplomacy = Personal Gravity!

4. Emotional Intelligence = *A New Memory Bank!*

To charge your emotional intelligence with **PERSONAL GRAVITY** at the mental level of your self-growth means to raise your self-consciousness, monitoring it digitally now. You need to considerably enrich your intelligence and diplomatically monitor your emotion + manners,. Your bad habits need to be grounded and memory renewed.

New times = *New Self-Structure* + *New Memory Base* = *New Knowledge* + *New Values* = *New Inner Space* = **An Acculturated Self.**

Due to the avalanche of information that we process now, our minds get clogged, and the mental turmoil damages our emotional make-up. We become impatient, de-focused, and irritable. It means that we need to manage the mental information that we get with the emotional diplomacy restrictions. Extreme emotions shorten our lives. *"Intelligent people live longer."* (*N. P. Bekhtereva. a famous Russian neuroscientist*)

The artificial mind is acting quickly and precisely in any emotional situation, and we need to urgently follow suit. (*See Part Two - The Sense of Measure*) So, we must sift the information for its validity, and enrich the **AWARE ATTENTION BANK.** The deposits into this bank must be made in five realms of knowledge - *physical, emotional, mental, spiritual, and universal.* We have no luxury any more to store the information unconsciously. Therefore, we need to optimize and strategize the in-coming information into *the new physical, emotional, mental, spiritual, and universal* **memory-compartments.**

Be wise! Optimize, Strategize, and Actualize !

Artificial intelligence is merging with human intelligence now, and it cleanses it of the centuries-long human negligence! The present-day revolutionary times require well-trained, emotionally diplomatic self-conscious professionals, able to process knowledge. in all levels.

So, Be Consciously Fast! Adjust to the Digital Mind-Monitoring Gust!

5. Mental + Emotional Self-Renaissance

Emotional Diplomacy and Artificial Intelligence need to merge not only in terms of information sorting out and the creation of a more evolved **human hybrid**. We need *the Emotional Diplomacy Skills* that we lack **to be coded into our future robot-friends** that will come handy in the situations when our mood might sag or we get depressed, overwhelmed, upset, etc. **Robots will help us get stabilized**. Hopefully, the Auto-Suggestive programming will become digitized and spontaneous in its robotic psychological application. It must be short and rhyming because the rhyming word is the short-cut to the **brain + mind sync** that yet remains a scientific tabula rasa of a mind-boggling value.

Putting the left-right brains in sync must be better connected to the **Master Computer Link!**

Also, the mind must be changing the brain, our biological computer, by *modifying the programs*, or its hardware, *content-wise and speed-wise.*

The memory bank will be a holistically modified emotional operational system that we need desperately. We'll gradually develop the stable ability **to ground our negative emotions properly** then and there, and we'll be better able to switch the aware attention in the positive, constructive direction, especially for business and love purposes.

Being godly in a godless world will be finally monitored!

In the same way as we feel healthier if we step barefoot on the grass , the sand, the ground, the river etc. because we are grounding the negative energies inside and feel **ONENESS** with the Mother Earth, we'll feel much more mentally enhanced if we someday manage to establish a **MAN'S MIND + UNIVERSAL MIND** link.

I wish I could live then in the unaswerable When!

Don't Be Life Static. Be Life-Diplomatic!

Section 2

(Self-Installation Stage of a Self-Renaissance Sage)

Being the Best

is

a Tough Test!

A. Einstein's mother kept telling her son,

"Keeping busy brings blessings!"

(Rule # 42 of Self-Renaissance)

I'm Physically Fit, Emotionally Up-Beat, Mentally Rich, and Spiritually Free;

I'm a New Me!

'It's Not Enough to Be the Best; Be the Only!" (*Steve Jobs*)

(Best Photos, The Internet Collection)

Live in Your Own Standards, not in People's Grandeurs!

1. Those Who Defy the Common Gravity- Fly!

There is a common opinion that wealth gives class, grace, and stature. Wealth surely helps, but **a great personality and wealth go together** only when being a great person, you are doing what only you can do. A person becomes unbeatable on the way of **realization of his /her exceptionality** because he / she gets charged from the Above with **the spirit of a winner**, sure of the absolute necessity to realize the ideas that he channels in connection with the *Universal Informational Field.*

Only the person who is on the Self-Renaissance path has such perceptive, goal-focused mind and **characterful guts.** It does not work in a reverse way because the reverse way does not develop a person's **SELF-CONSCIOUSNESS!** The other way is the dead end that does not make a person self-realized spiritually. He / she does not manage to obtain *"**spiritualized intelligence**"* that propels a person to the stars.

Those who defy the common gravity – fly; those who crawl -die!

The result is always the same, according to the British philosopher *David Eike*: ***"We have giants of money and intellect, but "pigmies of spiritual qualities."*** Only, developing self-consciousness can one obtain true spiritual maturity, personal integrity, **emotional gravity** and **charismatic magnetism.** These are the prerequisites of high self-consciousness – **the outcome of anyone's well-lived life**. Only having developed high self-consciousness, can you expand your personal informational field and get connected to *the Universal Informational Field,* or ***"The Source"*** *(Dr. Wayne Dyer)* and integrally connect yourself into a whole human being of Steve Job's type. So, the Paradigm of Self-Installation remains to be exceptional.

Body + Spirit + Mind + Self-Consciousness + Super-Consciousness = Self-Renaissance!

2. Be a Maker of Life; Be a Jeff Bezos Type!

(An Inspirational Booster)

To launch your mind into an avalanche of dollars

You must follow up those

Who know how to put the brace

On the money's interface!

True, money makes a lot of sense

In our life's existential essence!

But it stays only with those

Who let it work and repose!

In banks, in stocks,

Or in our grandmothers' socks!

To be under the monitory Sun,

You must moderate your immediate gratification fun!

Not to trash your cash and not to disrespect

Your life's financial aspect!

Be your money's best friend,

But never let it prevent

You from giving and seeing that money is but the means

To raise your happiness and health twins!

So, rack your brains to find the ways

To give your money more space!

But do not overdo with money accumulation ado!

Defy the gravity

Of its self-ruining vanity!

Don't let the money get stiff,

And do not whine, "I could do it, if…"

Neither fall into getting overjoyed

With bridging of the money's void!

Get rich in your mind first

To satisfy your money thirst!

Feel rich

Even when richness is out of reach!

Feeling dictates being, being depends on seeing,

Seeing resides in doing!

Doing makes you movable

And money-making doable!

So, be a maker of life

Be a man of Jeff Bezos type!

Try like him to unify

All your goals and fly!

(Rule # 43 of Self-Renaissance)

Holistically Knowledge-Steer; Your Mind is Your Career!

3. Mental Sanity is Based on Emotional Self-Gravity!

The traditional understanding of religion and its dogmas is enlightened now with **the informational essence of the Universe** which we are tapping into for a better understanding of **WHO** we are and **HOW** the universal force that we all call God is governing our thoughts. The structure of the universal life that is reflected in the perfect structure of our bodies makes us go beyond the terrestrial limits of understanding of life and living. **Our mental excellence is boundless!**

(Body+ Spirit+ Mind) + **(Self-Consciousness + Universal Consciousness)**

.We are energy and information connected to both - the Earth and the Universe, and the gravitational force of both is affecting the unity of the **body + spirit+ mind,** making us live by the Cosmic Laws that we do not consciously consider. We are developing from simple to the complex, from entropy to new energy of life construction, moving to the upper levels of actionable thought evolution, one step at a time. A person is healthy if *the energy of the body and the energy of his self-consciousness are in* sync.

Naturally, if we are not on the self-growth path and are NOT consciously moving toward higher levels of self-creation, we fall into a disbalance at the *physical, emotional, mental, spiritual, and universal levels.* We become disoriented and moneyless!

So, **the mental growth is multi-dimensional,** too! *(See the Excellence Award winner" Living Intelligence of the Art of Becoming!")* When you are leading your life / business in the conscious way, **building up your intelligence in all ten realms,** you are building up life / business *in sync with the universal laws of creation.*

Mental Gravity leads to Success without Any Materialistic Vanity!

4. Concluding the Mental In-put

Concluding my mental in-put,

I ask you all to display your kindness out-put!

I call on you not to waste

Your mind + heart's base!

Don't grudge

To display your intelligence and kindness at large!

Your life's boomerang range

Will finally change

Because kindness and mindedness

Will remove all biasness!

Without our true sincerity

There's no common unity

Of the heart and the mind

In One mutual wind!

Only the heart and the mind in sync

Create a Happy Life's Link!

"Awaken your evolutionary potential and activate your super-human capabilities."(*Gregg Braden*)

(Rule # 44 of Self-Renaissance)

Be Immune to the Poison of Life, Be Smart and Intellectualize Your Heart!

5. Have No Strife in Your Professional Life!

The Reminder: Having completed **the Mental level** of reviewing *"Self-Renaissance"* in the essential vistas of intelligence , or at the end of the day, conduct a quick **SELF-SCANNING,** following the evolutionary paradigm, as you've done it above.

Expand your intelligence with the technological miracles!

Self-Synthesis starts with making up the **HOLISTIC PICTURE OF SELF** every day, working on your Self-Installation objectively and honestly. *Your professional growth depends a lot of your emotional fort.* The heart and the mind must be in sync at your work's link.

Self-Analysis should be conducted as a quick review of *your physical, emotional, mental, spiritual, and universal realms* of life. This **SELF X-RAYING** will show you what strata of your professional life you succeed or fail in. *You need to give the world the best you have!* So, be the best in your professional quest!

Analyze 1) *your health* and the physical activity. **2)** *the attitude to yourself* and the people around you, **3)** *new knowledge* that you enriched your intelligence with and the strategic plan of action, leading to your full professional Self-Installation; 4) *your faith* and following its messages in action. *5) commitment to your exceptionality.*

Final Self-Synthesis – Completing the **SELF-ASSESSMENT**, give yourself grades for each level separately and figure out the average grade for the day. *(3.5 /,4 etc.)* In other words, you must assess the ability *to manage yourself* in the changing reality.. Self-scanning, as a general, objective vision of Self is very beneficial if you visualize the paradigm of self-creation holistically and walk yourself up to the top of your life.. It's like looking at the mirror of your soul to be consoled..

Live with the Zest! Success is Abreast!

Emotionally Balance Your Mind's Sight.

(Best Photos, Internet Collection)

Mental Sanity is the Core for the
Emotional Gravity!

Stage Two

(Self-Monitored Stage for a Self-Renaissance Sage)

Emotional Dimension - Self-Monitoring

Synchronize Your Life with the Mind + Heart Drive!

Use the Auto-Suggestive Programming for the Emotional Self-Refining!

Be More Aware of Your Digitally Monitored Emotional Soft-Ware!

Self-Culture Means Holistically Based Self-Acculturation!

Self-Renaissance

Form   +   Content

(Body+ Spirit+ Mind) + (Self-Consciousness + Universal Consciousness)

Living Intelligence   +   Enlightened Self-Consciousness = A Whole Self!

- - - - - - - - - - - - - - - -

5. *Universal Realm = Self- Acculturated;*

4. *Spiritual Realm   =   Self- Realized!*

3. *Mental Realm   =   Self-Educated;*

2. *Emotional Realm = Self-Controlled;*

1. *Physical Realm   = Self-Aware*

The Harmony of the Heart + Mind Sync is the
Main Goal of the Emotional + Mental link =
Personal Gravity =   Self-Consciousness

The process of raising Self-Consciousness is very complicated and must be consciously monitored by everyone of us, willing to upgrade their physical, emotional, mental, spiritual, and universal status in life.

The New Culture of Self-Acculturation is in

Self-Consciousness Formation.

Section 1

(Personal Diplomacy is an Emotional Self-Management)

Life Gaining

is in the

Emotional Gravity

and

Self-Taming!

Use the present-day technology to maintain your

Self-Monitored Inner Ecology!

Self-Corruption Starts with the Emotional Disruption!

Immediate Gratification is Resisted by the Mental Elation!

1. Emotional Gravity without Self-Vanity!

At the emotional level of our Self-Renaissance managing our emotions becomes imperative because at present we experience a huge disconnection between the heart and the mind that are governed by strong and destructive **SELF-VANITY** that pushes a person to react to self-gratification whims then and there.

Being too self-conscious makes you very obnoxious!

Being self-conscious generates the disconnection with the Universal Intelligence breaking its main link - **INTUITION + CONSCIENCE**. This link is our main indicator of the right and wrong. Acting consciously with the reasoning that is conscience -based is the main Emotional Diplomacy *"objectivizer."* Being compulsive, in contrast, is disregarding the inner voice of reason. Unfortunately, it is happening all over. People prostitute themselves for money and love, or for what they call love, silencing their conscience that later dies out for good.

Unfortunately, pretentiousness, fake straightforwardness, and open aggressiveness characterize women now more than men. The features of both sexes are interchangeable now, and that, according to *Dr. Bell ,* is *"an evolutionary thing"*. But both are willing to provide *"the internal massage"* then and there with the sex intention that is undiplomatically bare. We do sometimes talk about the romantic side of love and sex manners for commercial reasons, but we don't follow them de facto.

When I'm writing about different aspects of the *Emotional Diplomacy,* I mean a willful, conscious, and consistent acculturation of the intellect, emotions, and manners that are the basis of the **EMOTIONAL GRAVITY** in a person. Lack of it becomes the most destructive pattern of behavior that is sowed in the brains and the hearts of young, inexperienced boys and girls who take it as a norm.

So, We Reap What We Sow! Oh! Oh! Oh!

2. Be Life-Diplomatic, Not Chaotic or Self-Growth Static!

In every book on **Self-Resurrection**, *(See Book Rationale above)* I'm talking about our **spiritualized intelligence** that is inseparable with the **EMOTIONAL DIPLOMACY SKILLS.** These skills must be developed in us as early as possible because they secure our inner equilibrium by <u>synchronizing the form and the content</u> of our lives in the conscious and holistic way.

FORM + CONTENT

(Body+ Spirit+ Mind) + **(Self-Consciousness + Universal Consciousness)**

The Auto-Suggestive Programming is, in fact<u>, the method of dealing with emotional impulsivity</u> by inspiring your **Self-Renaissance-geared infinity!** The time for our commonsense justification , used as an excuse for making the same mistakes and being in the turmoil of the same weakness, *"Nobody is perfect."* is an outdated lame excuse now.

<u>You must be on the track of making yourself as perfect as possible</u>!

You are competing with the Artificial Intelligence! So*,* open the window into your new thinking and flood it with digitally renewed creative energy of love for God, life, and yourself.

The process of creating a **NEW YOU** must be conscious, objective, language and emotions controlled and governed by the new **LAWS OF GRACE:** The grammar of the religious perception of life now is in the unanimity of our perception of God and the present-day godliness.

Our common perception of God is <u>scientifically enriched</u>, and it needs to be reasoned out in unity with the Universal Intelligence, the **MASTER MIND** that is governing our lives irrespective of our different religious affiliation. Let me repeat it,

In God's Account, We All Count!

3. Life-Revising is in the Holistic Self-Synchronizing!

As is noted above, life-gaining is in the technologically enhanced **SELF-ACCULTURATION** which is in the accumulation of emotional **GRAVITY** and **SELF -SANITY.** You should be modelling your life in the emotional realm with the clear-cut awareness of the Universal gift of life, granted to you from the Above. Therefore, your Self-Renaissance in life must be based on the realization of your **EXCEPTIONALITY.**

Personal Gravity is the core of the Emotional Sanity!

Super level	Super-Consciousness	Self-Salvation
Macro level	Self- Consciousness	Self-Realization
Mezzo level	Mind	Self- Installation
Meta level	Spirit	Self-Monitoring
Mini level	Body	Self-Awareness

Delve into your emotional midst and display your gravity width!

Form   +   Content

(Body+ Spirit+ Mind) + **(Self-Consciousness + Universal Consciousness)**

Living Intelligence   + Enlightened Self-Consciousness = Personal Gravity!

Anything that happens consistently gets linked!

Only accumulating *emotional gravity in every dimension* can you stabilize your life and manage to instill order in it *physically, emotionally, mentally, spiritually, and universally.* So, at any moment of your life - joyful or hopeless, remember the King Solomon's rule of **SELF-GRAVITY,** "It too Shall Pass!"

Emotional Gravity is the Basis for Mental Sanity!

4. Integrity and Uprightness

We need a lot of guidance

In integrity and up-rightness!

But don't expect it to arrive

From the Above drive!

It comes only from outside in

And it requires a lot of discipline!

Reading, meditating, and re-forming

Are very re-directing and transforming.

 But what works best

Is a constant will-power fest!

For happiness is not the perfect good

That lulls our appetite's mood,

"It's an object of naught still

That can lull a man's will."

We need to restore

The inner Christ's temple at the core!

The core is in our hearts

That need to live at peace with the guts!

To be beautiful when you are stupid and young

Is a naturally enjoyable fun.,

But being aristocratic when you are wise and old

Requires working on a special mold!

And if you hadn't trained your will

To be patient, strong, and still,

The needed integrity and uprightness fix

Would never get rooted in your PERSONAL MATRIX !

The soul gets inevitably eroded,

And, hence, a person's life becomes corroded.

We get caught in a downward spiral,

The escape from which is always viral!

Thus, being godly, loving, and kind

Must always be on the mind,

While trying to be perfectly perfect is unrealistic

If not self-sadistic!

Only trying to be good and give one five

Is what you can always derive!

So, listen to your sincere voice within;

It's your inner twin!

Without it, your solid personal intelligence

Is of a pointless relevance.

(Rule # 45 of Self-Renaissance)

Let's Level by Level, enforce Self-Gravity without any Physical, Emotional, Mental, Spiritual, and Universal Vanity!

5. Remove the Synrom of the "Left Unsaid" Mind-Form!

There are pages written about the necessity to forgive and get rid of the burden of self-guilt and inner discomfort. I think that very often we are unable to forgive because we are holding back in the heart the words of clarity that were never told due to the emotiobal disbalance but that keep bothering us. These words are like a wall between us and the people who we were not sincere with about something still bothering us.

We need to remove the syndtrom of the left unsaid words before it might become too late , as it often does. Unfortunately, lack of sincerity and Emotional Diplomacy Skills of which **PERSONAL GRAVITY** is the most vital one, we keep justifying ourselves for not saying these words. **Personal vanity must be finally managed by self- gravity.**

Sincerity and authenticity are the pilas of personal gravity!

We dismiss the unsaid words at the moment that might have healed the situation if they had been said. We hold back sincere talking, thinking that our straightforwardness will hurt the person who these sincere words are mentally directed to. Then these words start rotting inside, polluting our bodies, hearts, and minds.The situation must be surgically and diplomatically resolved to ground the misunderstanding then and there. *"There are two ways out in every bad situation - a good one and a better one!"* (Jewish wisdom)

There are many different *Cause-Effect* disbalances that we generate in an impulsive state, allowing the unconscious mind to act in a habitual, reactive way. Only *awareness of the negative consequences of the unsaid words* will help ground the negative emotions then and there.

Life is Terminal. Don't Carry Your Burden Interminally!

6. Be Emotionally Up-beat but Stay in Your Gravitational Seat!

Why should you bother

When you are at the life's tether?

Why not stand at its abyss

As a stoical Mister or Miss

Who keeps saying to himself and you,

"Don't make much fuss about any life's ado!"

Every down will pass

With its next upcoming positive mass!

All you have to admit

Is the power of the Almighty "It!"

The Sun will still shine,

Whether you frown or smile!

The wind will yet blow

Whether you die or remain to flow!

And there'll still be a lot of misconception

Of your life's perception

By those who are close and those that are far,

Observing and judging you from afar!

What do they all know

About your life's flow?

So, what's the point of obsessing

Over your life's processing

 The present whines and tears

 Your smiles, and fears?

They'll all vanish

As the evolutionary garnish!

 Learn to be stoically bold -

 Fit in the new life's mold!

The Fractal of Emotional Diplomacy is based on the Balanced Normalcy!

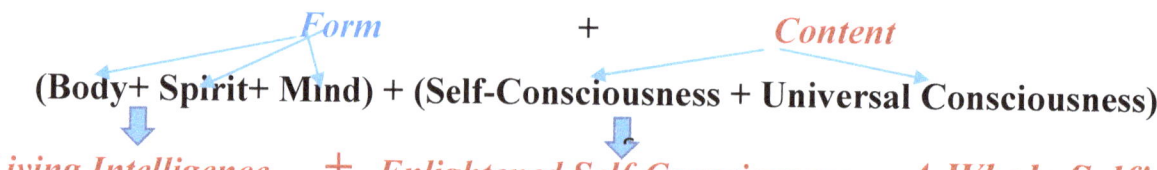

Form + *Content*

(Body+ Spirit+ Mind) + (Self-Consciousness + Universal Consciousness)

Living Intelligence + *Enlightened Self-Consciousness = A Whole Self!*

(See the book "Soul-Refining" -www.language Fitness .com)

Self-Renaissance is the Faith-Relationship with Yourself!

*In any negative situation, it's vital to **immediately ground your negative emotions** and calm down because calmness makes the gravitation of the negativity conscious and therefore, controlled. You'll manage to establish the emotional order and illuminate the impulsive chaos that ruins **the mind + heart connection**, essential in any communication. Anything that happens consistently gets linked!*

(Rule # 46 of Self-Renaissance)

Form + Content of Life in Twine is the Essence of Your New Life's Paradigm!

Secton 2

In Our Love-Search, We Need a Lot of Mental Watch!

Don't Be Love-Static; Be Love-Diplomatic!

Love is a self-sactrificing feeling of good actions dealing!

"Be the teacher of your heart,

but don't let your Heart become your Teacher!"

(Japanese Proverb)

Love Needs Emotional Gravity to be Instilled in the Character Field.

Let's Search for Love without Inhibition

(*Beenjamin Victor, a great American Sculptor*)

And Procreate this Feeling as a Mission!

1. Synchronize Your Life with the Love-Smart Drive!

Love is the Self-Renaissance basic stuff! Love is also the best response to the question **Why You Are?** The essential **LOVE SKILLS** are grace and nobility – the skills that are instilled in us since early childhood by the parents and through the fairy tales. Love must enlighten all five stages of Self-Renaissance in which you fall under the divine and objective judgement of Self and your partner.

That's why one of the main ideas of this book is being committed to Self-Renaissance by way of removing self-vanity and installing **heart + mind** unity. These are the prerequisites for *Emotional Diplomacy*. It can be accomplished, accumulating love and noble gravity in the heart and the mind. Unfortunately, love has become too **IMPULSIVE** and **IMPERSONAL.** It has lost its authenticity and a deep magnetic power of a truly uniting sacredness and grace. People talk a lot about the love for God but display no grace in their speech and faith.

To be inwardly with God, be a man /woman of your word!

Love still remains our main stimulus in life, our gulp of fresh air when we are suffocating from game-paying, cheating, shamelessness and sex-relativeness. Unfortunately, lack of the emotional gravity kills the ability to love, generating loveless, quick-fix relationships. If you want to stand out in life and make a difference, you need to begin connecting your mind with the heart and become love-smart! A love partner is your personal choice but be sure he / she has a worthy voice. If your partner supports mutual Self-Renaissance, race, sex-orientation, or religious affiliation does not matter; his / her self-consciousness does!

Intellectualize Your Heart and Emotionalize the Mind! Be One of a Kind!

2. Love Energy is in Inner Synergy!

So, your intellect should become profoundly enriched to be emotionally inclusive. Your **mind+ heart** link must become your **LOVE ANCHOR** in any life-challenging situation at home, at work, anywhere. To begin with, you must be aware of your emotions, both positive and negative, and this mindfulness will help you ground the negative impulses then and there. To help you synchronize yourself holistically, visualize the fractal formula of your inner unity that will help you in establishing solid **SELF-GRAVITY** as your love anchor.

(Body + Spirit + Mind) + (Self-Consciousness + Universal Consciousness)

In my book "***Love- Ecology***", I review love in five dimensions: *physical, emotional, mental, spiritual, and universal*, and you might want to do that yourself when you feel doubtful and love-depleted. When you are upset, become consciously aware of the fact that love, like everything else in life, is of the vibrational character, and after a bad moment, a good one will inevitably arrive. The same goes about being too ecstatic and overly romantic about love. Delusionary daydreaming must be self-monitored. Love is the feeling that envelopes us with equanimity. So, induct, **Equanimity is me; equanimity is my philosophy!**

We are restless and disbalanced when something is wrong on the love horizon. Once, everything gets back on the love track, we get calm, balanced, creative, and happy again because, in the most natural way, your *hearts* and minds find their mutual way! The most damaging and love-diminishing thing is the heart - mind disconnection. That is why when we are away from the loved ones, prompted by the intuition, we call them and thus, we put our minds and hearts in sync.

(Rule # 47 of Self-Renaissance)

The Heart and Mind in Sync Resolve Any Conflict in a Blink!

3. Be the Conductor of Your Emotional Factor!

To have pleasant love emotions is a job, to have no emotions is nonsense! Our experience proves that love turns into hatred very easily, but it happens if we do not control our emotions consciously. Love is he most natural state of wholeness – *physical, emotional, mental, spiritul and universal normalness.* That's why love has the greatest gravitational and inspirational value and these ethical precepts of love must be our Self- Educational Stuff! in schools and in a family life.

The brain + the heart manages and masters the Love Art!

Conscious emotional control means *being aware of both negative and positive emotions* and not allowing negative emotions take the upper hand in your life. Don't try to be loving forcefully, and do not depend of anyone's emotional assessment of you, either. Your solar plexus is the center of your solar system. To calm yourself down, put your left hand there when you get into any negative field that might de-magnetize your system. Keep your hand on the solar plexus while talking to a negative person, or anyone who is tongue-lashing you. Thus, you will heighten your emotional awareness and protect yourself from reacting to the negative words, directed at you. Self-awareness is key to Emotional Diplomacy! Remember, everything has its own rhythms: digestion, blood pressure, pulse rate, and a body temperature. You are the one in charge of the fluctuations in your solar system. Your cells will follow your orchestration! Be a great conductor of them! Your auto-suggestive programming with the help of conscious breathing will soon become an Emotional Diplomacy Skill with you.. Use any self-induction (*e.g.* **Life is tough, but I'm tougher***!*) to boost your self-liking which, no doubt, will be mounting in you in the process of your conscious Self-Renaissance. *To be inspired, be self-inspiring!*

(Rule # 48 of Self-Renaissance)

Never Lose the Sight of Your Divine Might!

4. Auto-Suggestive Meditation for Love-Elation

" *Love is written into our genetic Code. Loving another, you are on service to others.* Seek the heart of the Self!" *(David Wilcock)* With the help of simple inspirational **LOVE / SELF- LOVE HYPNOSIS**, you can help yourself or anyone up-lift the spirit or sculpture the sagging self-image. Helping someone *just* **change the pronoun "I "** *to* **"you.**" *In this case, stand behind a person and put the hands on his shoulders at the spots .describes below.*

1. Cross your arms as if hugging yourself on the shoulders so that the centers of your palms that represent the *solar plexus* in your body could lay on the *edges of your shoulders*, on their rounding parts. These are the spots of love!

2. Now, embrace yourself in thus fashion most lovingly. Then, start moving your hands slowly down your arms, saying to yourself the following booster:

Auto-induction: I love myself *(you)* *(breathe in)* – **p**ause - the way I am!*(you are -(breathe* out)

3. When your hands come to the point where *both palms meet*, make a short pause and say inwardly to yourself.

Auto- induction: If any one doesn't like me, *(breathe in -****Pause*)*

4. *Next, shake off your hands vigorously*, thus removing any negative thoughts or feelings that you might have harbored against yourself or other people that may be having grudges against you and say: *Auto- induction*: It's his or her problem, not mine! *(breathe out -****Relax*** *– shake off your hand several times, imagining* the negative emotions that you ground .with these gestures. *Picture the face of a person who might not like you for some reason. Wish him / her well.* Be kind to the unkind. Be One of a kind!

5. Conclude self-inducting with: I know who I am! I am a strong, calm, and determined owner of my firm will.

I can…; I want to …; And I will…! *(Say what you need to do.)*

I'm becoming better and better etc. with each coming minute, hour, day.

Hurrah to Me, Hurrah!

5. Don't Evil-Sprout - Breathe in and Breathe out!

(Do the Auto-Suggestive coding with any mindset that resonates with you.)

Breathe in a cold emotional breeze,

Breathe out a warm intellectual heath.

Start your self-reform,

Put on a Self-Renaissance uniform!

Force a smile

On your face for a while.

Let it stay there as a mask even through

It's a difficult task!

Learn to say, "No!" to your emotional whims

And uncontrolled below!

Zip your mouth

For the cloudy words directed at your spouse!

If you do not want to synchronize

With the predetermined vice,

Stay away from the temptation

That is thrown at you in variation!

Everything in life's sight

Is tricky and tight.

To find a wider way,

You need to struggle every day!

So, set the control

Over your God-given soul!

Be a good humankind –

One with the Universal Mind!

Make Emotional Self-Discipline

Your Life's Main Gene!

What you can be,

You must be!

What you can have,

You must have!

What you can do,

You must do!

So, be, have, and do

To qualify for a self-guru!

(Rule # 49 of the Emotional Diplomacy)

I Can! I Want to...! And I Will!

That's My Life Motto still!

6. Our Human Entirety is Based on Personal Gravity!

In sum, **to beat the self-defeat**, your spirit needs to be "ensured" with the help of sci-tech application in your smart phone. The contradictory impulses of the subconscious mind that dictates you the impulsive actions-reactions must be numbed down by the conscious mind . So, upload any inspirational mind-set to remind yourself of the fractal unity that you need to preserve. It becomes a piece of cake for you to put yourself together because every new programming of the mind deletes the harmful habits and impulsive reactions in the sub-conscious memory department. Keep your **AWARE ATTENTION** on alert any time a negative emotion hits your body. You'll finally manage to accumulate. **INNER GRAVITY** of the Emotional Diplomacy.

Personal gravity kills stupid, impulsive vanity!

Personal gravity is your emotional anchor, and it can be attained only if you strengthen your willpower and up-grade the level of your bioenergy consciously in **a holistically aristocratic, self-loving way** .Also, you need to take a vow that every time you fight with the loved ones that , you will use nice words at the end to obliterate the conflict for these words might be the last ones we had a chance to say to each other. When my Polish grandmother died, I was only six years old, but if I had a fight with my younger brother, she wouldn't let me go to bed without making up with him. She always said, "**Don't go to bed being angry with the ones you love. Our loved ones are not duplicated by God for us , and they can be taken from us any minute if we do not show love for them. Keep peace with them to have peace inside.**" I made this rule my Emotional Diplomacy tool!

Be Always Reserved in Your Self-Respected Aristocratic Fort!

Emotional Diplomacy for Family-Management

Family Gravity
is in
Love Trinity!

Any relationship is a variable reality, not an absolute one.

A cloudless relationship is not possible but sustaining the emotional climate in it is your responsibility!

(Rule # 50 of the Emotional Diplomacy)

Exemplify the self-sacrificing love as your primary mission
in a family of no love fiction!

Love Pollution has become Our Common Social Constitution!

We are All One in the Embrace of Love!

(The Best Photo – The Internet Collection)

Build up the Golden Section of Your Love-Reflection!

1. The Authenticity of Love is the Educational Stuff!

To begin with, <u>Love Skills</u> need to be instilled in kids both by the example of the parents' respectful relationship and the images of **LOVE MANAGEMENT** Skills, installed by the stories of true love from classic literature, wonderful, love-imbuing movies, and beautiful music that should fill the audio-world of the young minds. The psychologically grounded knowledge of <u>Self-Management + Love-Management</u> must be in the background of any subject teaching by the teaches whose hearts and minds are in sync, too. As Leo Vygotsky said,

<u>**"Don't teach just the subject. teach the whole person!"**</u>

I'm not going to quote here a well-known definition of a family love that *the Bible* provides, accentuating the meaning of *the Trinity* in love, *not as a man, a woman, and a child* , but as <u>God + a man + a woman.</u> It *is a love-gluing trinity* that justifies itself in many God-abiding families governed by the strong bonds of new family values.

(Body+ Spirit+ Mind) + **(Self-Consciousness + Universal Consciousness)**

For centuries, the idea of the sacredness of a family life was dominant in our minds, but it has **a new aura of social acceptance** now that we must respect whether we like it or not. And again, *the level of self-consciousness, a person's intelligence , and a respectful love for a partner* should be the Emotional Diplomacy norms in any family unity. The rule, " ***Don't judge, not to be judged*** " must finally get rooted in us.

The process of tongue-taming should not be stuck in computer gaming!

The society's judgement and boundless talks of a diminishing character in mass media lower these people in their self-consciousness.

(Rule # 51 of the Emotional Diplomacy)

Respect is Me; Respect is My Philosophy!

2. No Fracture in Holistic Family Structure

There is another stigma that needs to be removed from the surface of a family life. It is **a deep sense of responsibility** for the life of the person who shares your space and time in life on the one hand, and the kids in a family, on the other. It's love-worthy to be godly in a godless world!

The shallow rule, " *No one is obligated to anyone!*" that is often heard in the situation that demand from one of the partners display *aristocratic nobility, compassion, consideration and humility.* This is a lame excuse of someone's weakness and a sure proof of his / her **conscience sickness,** conscience being our direct line to God! We know that love is blessed from the Above, but we forget that to be registered in the Universal Love Court , we need to have **INTUITION** and **CONSCIOUENCE** aboard. Instead of being reactive, become responsibly pro-active! Our loved ones and especially children should not be **heart-broken** because they immediately become **mind-broken**, and, consequently, the **heart + mind unity** that I'm advocating for in every book on self-creation.

Only with this link at work, can both love partners recognize each other **EXCEPTIONALITY** and **sustain the on-going competition of the personalities** in the challenging reality. In fact, self-realization with a successful outcome is a tough task, and it needs a holistic preservation of the family structure OR the love structure for support. I realize now that we can hardly be happy unless we build up solid **WHOLENESS** in the relationship with each other in all five levels - *physical, emotional, mental spiritual, universal* and erect the common love refuge, not a sandcastle. My first marriage failed because we clicked only on the first three levels. If you have the unity in five levels , there is solid hope.

The Stable State of Love is Governed Holistically from the Above!

3. A Family's Love Gravity

So, we must seriously **reconsider our attitude to the concept of a family in a new way** at the time of new love relationships that are becoming more and more digitized. The words about the importance of a family are heard in the churches and at the holiday tables as the banal tosts, but families fall apart just at the first signs of a husband's or a wife's cheating digressions.To break a family means to distroy the FAMILY'S LOVE GRAVITY that allows us to raise children in the atmosphere of the family emotional diplomacy, essential for the healthy growth of children. Men are hytorogenic creatures, created to impregnate other women and love, but not once. So, why do we forget about the nature of life and ruin the basis of *the family's integrity* just on the grounds of someone' change of the bed habits and preferences.

Marriage is an inspired decision made with the mind's precision!

A well-known *"Backlash Theory"* proves that if a woman who has discovered that her man cheated on her behaves calmly and understandingly, the man, who, at the start of his new relationship compares a new woman in the dis-favor of his wife *(or a new partner in a relationship)* will inevitably experience a backlash.

In three months or less, the man will start comparing his wife (*a partner*) in her favor, realizing that women are all physically and emotionally the same, and the sub-consciously formed family habits are much more stable. Men, normally, want to come back, but a betrayed woman plays the saddest tune on her violine. The result is always the broken hearts, and the kids' future life becomes messed up at every level. This behavior is unforgivable! A woman's haert + mind link must be prioritized here because she must consider the kids'psychological security first. *The vanity of self-worth is the secondary force here!.*

Relative Love is Not a Family's Glueing Stuff!

221

4. Love Energy is the Whole Brain's Synergy!

The importance of the language gravity was commented on above. Unfortunately, language profanity and rudeness in many families are appalling, and kids get indoctrinated with this family poisoning context. Our merging with the Artificial intelligence might be the light at the end of the tunnel in this respect because kids will follow the instructions of the robots much better. It will be a great blessing for parents .

I'd like to mention here the movie "**HER**" with two brilliant actors, *Joaquin Phoenix and Scarlett Johansson*, who managed to communicate to us the rainbow of sincerity and true sensuality in the hearts and minds of two beings – a human being and a machine They grow closer and closer inwardly during their operational communication, and eventually, they fall in love, totally grasping our attention and playing on our innermost soul cords. I'm not a prude, but the sacredness and real beauty of such symphony-like feelings of love are my stuff!. Hopefully, artificial intelligence will beautify our near future. with new love quality and authenticity, with reasoning and compassionate care. The Japanese people are applying such care already. I salute to them!

I also salute to Elon Musk for directing his genius to the human mind + heart unity now. This incredible endeavor will not only have a huge impact on the medical realms, but it will also help a human mind become more reasonable, conscious, and self-monitoring in every dimension of our evolutionary development, putting the whole brain synergy back in action - *physical + emotional + mental + spiritual + universal realms in sync!* **Love connects; hate disconnects!**

Such patches of the holistic authenticity of love leave us hopeful that love in its universal sense will embraces all the aspects of our life someday. Meanwhile, we need to raise our self-awareness and instill in our inner space *the unity of the hearts and minds* without which no emotional gravity can be accumulated.

Love's Bliss is Not a Myth!

5. Let's Not Be Too Hard on a Man's Heart! *(A Justification Poem)*

Let's not be too hard

On a man's heart,

        For men can hardly fall

        For one woman at all!

Once they get attached

To a marriage match,

        The Law of Attraction

        Takes turn to a subtraction!

The fluctuations of love friction

Change into the bursts of love fiction!

        The opposites attract and repulse

        This is the normal love pulse!

So, why give vows and empty promises

That go in reverse with the laws of the Universe.

        Let's take it for granted that love is alive

        Till we start moving apart in life!

When it occurs,

Don't turn the love's normal course!

        Leave it to come back

        On its initial track!

It'll happen by the Law of Magnetism,

If you don't rely on spiritualism!

Men need to impregnate many,

They cannot stand still and not feel!

So, let's look at love consciously and realistically

And be less oriented emotionally and mystically!

Love till a birch tree on the common grave

May be a true or a naïve love frame!

Focus on your own life's mission

And view love as the path to God for its submission!

Admire your man for his self-worth

And let him be your family's boss!

The light of evolving attitudes and behaviors will rein

in the heart + mind mutual gain!

Form   +   Content

(Body+ Spirit+ Mind) + (Self-Consciousness + Universal Consciousness)

Living Intelligence   + Enlightened Self-Consciousness = A Whole Self!

In Our Love-Search,

We Need a Lot of Mental Watch!

Unconditional Love is a Man's Stuff!

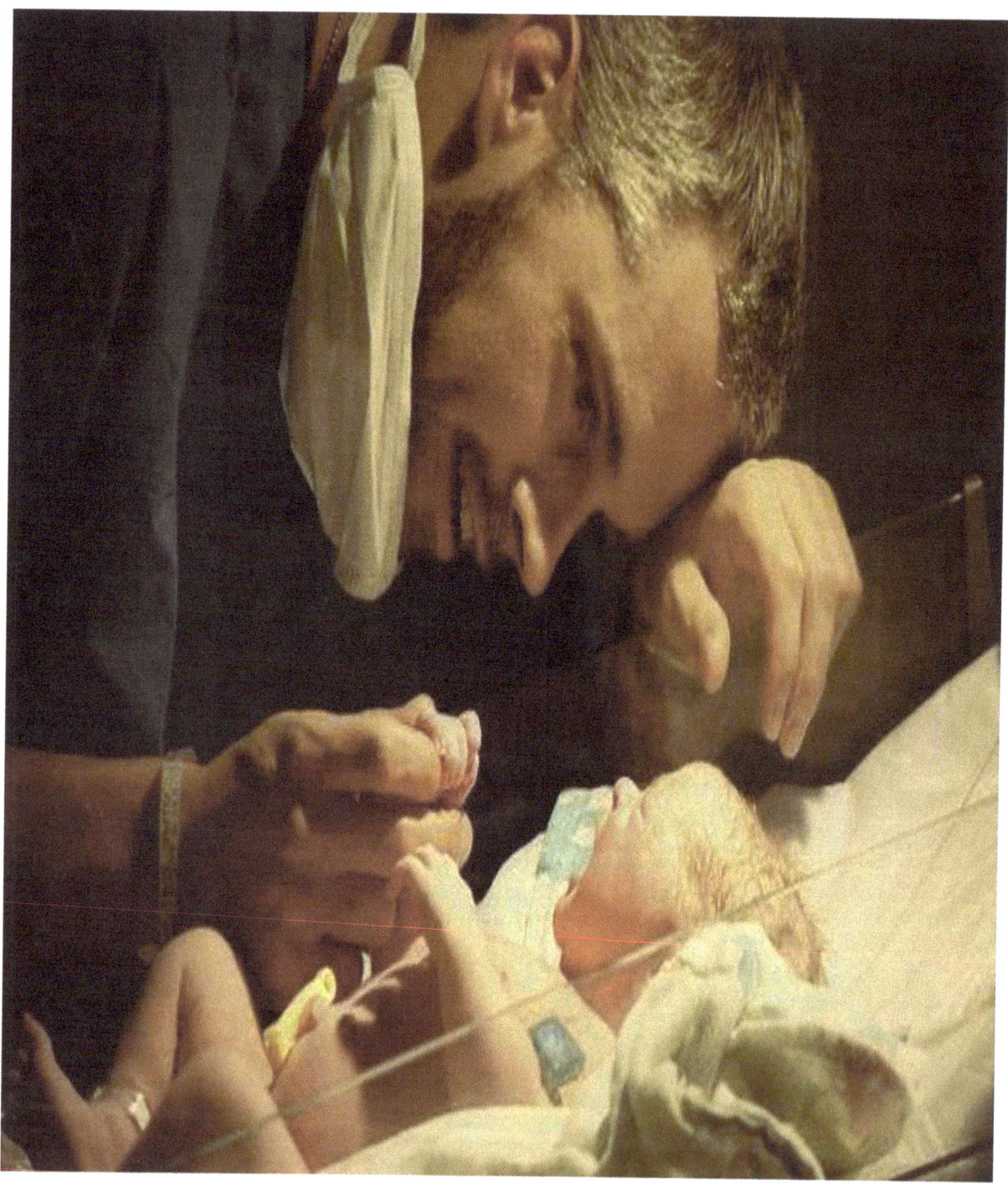

"A Man in a Family is Happiness."

(A Gergeon Proverb)

6. A Family's Emotional Diplomacy

Undeniably, the present-day life proves a vital significance of a person's *self-realization* that is always based on the expression of his / her **EXCEPTIONALITY** in life, to begin with. So, the choice of the **ONE** and the **ONLY** should start with X-raying *the one who touches your heart and mind in sync*, not just excites you physically.

Your love needs to be processed through all five levels, starting not with the physical one, but with the universal level that will ascertain if the person of your life choice has *any exceptional goals for self-realization* beyond the material ones and if you share them. In love function, self-worth of a person is the best attraction because it has the magnetic gravity of a worthy personality.

The essence of a **FAMILY's EMOTIONAL DIPLOMACY** is in the recognition of the partner's spiritual values, too. Then, if you recognize each other's exceptionality and spirituality and can wholeheartedly support and respect both of them, *your ambition to accomplish your unified goals will double,* and the outcome will be most successful one for both of you. Your heart + mind sync will strengthen this essential link! Also, learn to praise your second half for his / her smallest accomplishments or any signs of love and attention. *There should be no spiteful competition on the love mission!*

Don't take love for granted. It is God granted!

Next, analyze why you click mentally, emotionally and spark each other physically, and only then make the final decision that, hopefully, will help you stay together for years to come. It may sound idealistic, but it is the only way to stay together through thick and thin. Bur remember,

The Family that is Betrayed Has No Love Rebate!

7. What We Promise to Be Ultimate, Becomes Temporary!

I have verified my revelation of <u>the holistic value of love-management</u> through getting rid of my personal ignorance that brought to ruins my first marriage. It has thrived for twenty-five years at *the physical, emotional and mental levels* thanks to my <u>diplomatic attitude to my husband's exceptionality</u> and his natural for a man small digression.

My self-worth kept me sane because I knew that it's incredibly difficult for an intelligent and gifted man *(a TV director)* to find a woman who would have the package of qualities, enabling both of us to click on three levels that secured an unbreakable family unity for years. But immigration and mostly *the spiritual / religious polarity,* revealed in the USA *(my husband is Jewish, and I'm Russian)* did the inevitable. The upper two levels of the *spiritual and universal* magnetic values were not reached. I didn't know better then. The sacred truth of the Bible: <u>"A family, divided against itself falls"</u> proved its validity to me here..

So, <u>if the One and the Only was not selected in all five levels of life,</u> chances are the disconnection will inevitably occur at this level of the next. The two people begin to grow out of attachment and love for each other once they start sharing their bodies, the living space, and the time. It happens as a disappointment because there were blind expectations. Our sub-conscious mind prompts the pictures of a partner in marriage or a relationship, growing with you in a certain way.

We forget that <u>love needs constant refreshing of the expertise,</u> like we do it in our professional life. Love and marriage are the jobs that are based not on the expectations of joy and pleasure, but on a solid sense of responsibility to provide joy and pleasure for the each other in a family.

(Rule 51 of Emotional Diplomacy)

Love is Not a Habit; It's a Skill!

8. The Unity of the Minds and Hearts, Not the Butts, grows the Love Guts!

In sum, *consciousness of a man or a woman will gradually come to the forefront in a relationship. not his / her sexual preferences*. **SEX-CONSCIOUSNESS** is inseperable with a person's intelligence,. his / her inner freedon, self-confidence, and a strong sense of Self. Sex orientation is entirely a personal business, as well as a person's moral values and beliefs.

O**ne's exceptionality is not expressed through a sexual vanity.**

The person who knows who he is, would not be engagesd in gay parades or ugly shameless shows. Nor would a person with a developed self-consciousness demonstrate an aggravating human ability *to love negatively, with conditions and demands* that have mushroomed lately and that no psychiatrist can cure. Love skills are not a given!

A love-advanced person with the **EMOTIONAL DIPLOMACY SKILLS** of whatever sexual orientation can always demonstrate his mind, a unique vision of the reality, the ability to give and to forgive, to love and be loved in return. Making a show of one's love preferences demonstrates mass media's limitedness of intelligence and consciousness Love must be studied, respected, and learned. It's our main personal fort! Sex-consciousness must be the ultimate goal of such education. Being love-diplomatic means being aristocratic!

A love-diplomatic person will not judge anyone's choice in love. A person's self-worth is his /her main force. Emotinal diplomacy must be applied here much more than in any other area of our life. So, let's *change our tactics to enjoy peace practics!*

Love Grows Only in the Pure Mind's Soil, Not in the Perverted Sex Turmoil!

Emotional Diplomacy for Sex Gravity

Don't Dive

into Anyone's

Sex Life!

"A man who cannot give a woman anything always says that she wants too much".*(Edgar Cayce)*

"A man and a woman start cheating on each other when they get tired of changing the other." *(Carl Yung)*

To have the relationship built in stone, strengthen your Authenticity Bone!

(Rule # 52 of the Emotional Diplomacy)

Let's Find the Best in Each Other and Resist the Attitude" I'd rather..!"

Sex is an Art of Life; Let it Thrive!

You are Part Of Me; I'm Part of You!

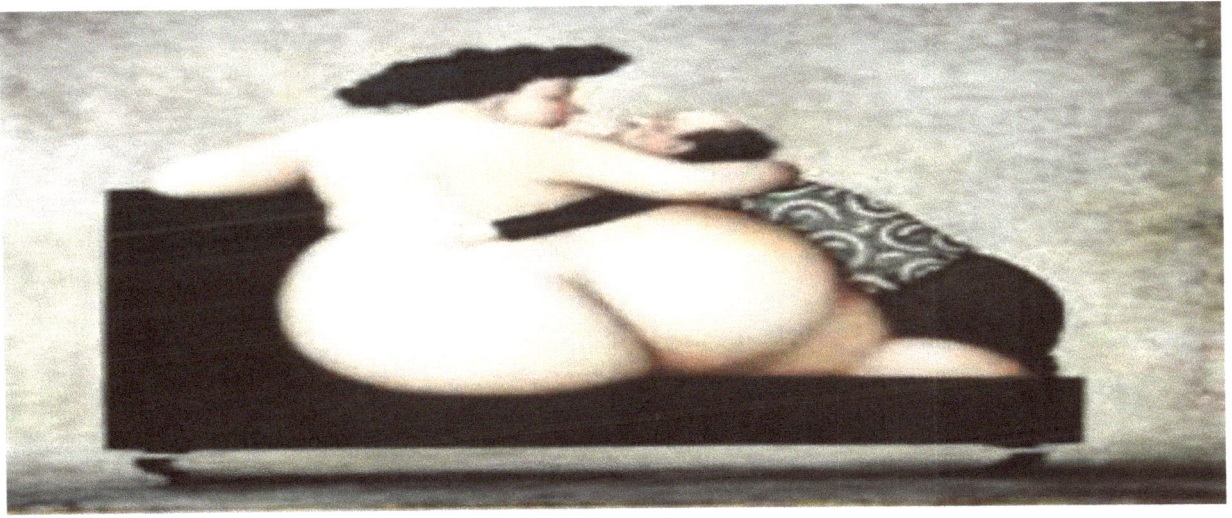

We are One Together!

1. Sex-Renaissance and Sex-Management

Sex is the fundamental biological feature of our existence. *Emotional Diplomacy* and **SEX-RENAISSANCE** are inseparable as the most beautiful features of life-management. Both are directly connected with the **CODEX Of LOVE-MAKING** that should be worked out by our psychologists and physiologists and presented in schools, not just as sex-education, but as an essential part of **LIFE-MANAGEMNT.**

It must be a broad subject, teaching young people different aspects of life and *conscious living*, with sex-education as a part of it. Early sex life destroys emotionally unstable girls and boys. That's why *Emotional Diplomacy* must be basic in sex-education because without it, sex becomes devoid of gravity and respectful sanity! **Sex-awareness** must be knowledge-based because without it, the effect of hormones on *the body and intelligence* of a person generate the dis-connection of the mind + heart link, essential in *Self-Renaissance.*

Cheating, game playing, and sex addiction turn sex into a fiction!

Young people should be taught the ways to manage their sexual impulses consciously. To return the sacred meaning of the basic life-creation phenomenon, education must instill the **EMOTIONAL DIPLOMACY GRAVITY** into the young souls. They will still be conditioned by the sex drive, but they'll become more able to control it consciously. At present, sex is too impulsive and de-graded in its life-producing value, and such situation keeps generating many traumas and broken lives. Studying *Emotional Diplomacy* will help our young people see sex not as the device to enslave the other, but as *the main energizer to keep us motivated in a personal self-growth.*

Be Immune to Any Toxic Spell; Sexually Stabilize Yourself!

2. Be a Sex-Gravity Guru. then Love will Gravitate to You!

We also need to be more considerate of the sex mood that is so different in men and women in order to develop the **SEX-GRAVITY** that is an essential skill of *Emotional Diplomacy* and which must not be based on guilt and fear.

"Guilt and fear are the controlling tools of the population, and sex is the main incentive of both." (Sadhguru)

If a woman's mind is often preoccupied with the sickness of a child or other problems, connected with the family's well-being, her fragile psychological state must be respected. Also, women tend to hurt a man's feelings . commenting on his sexual ability in a very disrespectful way, thus ruining the mind+ heart unity , if any, in the relationship .

Be tactful and diplomatic, not love-sporadic!

In the atmosphere of *toxic love*, when *ponography* is taking **70%** of the Internet trafic and sex orientation becomes relative, we stop considering diplomatic **SEX-MANAGEMENT** as an important defyning feature in a personality growth and the priority goal in *self-consciousness formation* that must be based on a controlled sex impulse and *a noble, graceful, and grateful treatment of a sex-partner.* The unhealthy treatment of the subject for centuries on end causes *the sex cells freeze or become unmanageable* in the cases of sex addiction or sex-perversion. History has left for us wonderful manuals on *the Art of Sex* that can easily be studies on the Internet to enrich our education not only sex-positions-wise, but , most-importantly, instilling in us the sacred piety of the sex-gift as the source of all creation.

Choreograph Your Personal Drive; Let the Other Party Sex-Thrive!

3. I Want to Be Your Last Love Stage!

(A Sincere Wish Disclosure)

I want you to be my last love stage

And you to become my love sage.

I need to co-feel and to co-guard,

And to never ask for love refund!

I look forward to living together not till death,

But to be delving in unity for inner soul's depth!

For shared knowledge and places,

For flights and new ideas' embraces.

For a glass of water and a pill,

If my health needs a refill.

In the Family Fort of our Love Age ,

I want you to be my last male / female stage!

Stop pretending to be loving without feeling love!

(See the lbook " Love- Ecology" ,2020),

The Authenticity of Love is a five-leveled Stuff!

(Rule 53 of Emotional Diplomacy)

Keep Privacy Within the Limits of Decency!

233

4. Don't Stereotype Love; Love is a Holistically Personal Stuff!

In love essense, <u>a man needs to be respected for his exceptionality</u>, and a woman must be loved for seeing it in him. However, we keep justifying ourselves for any relationship's or family discords. Our absolute ignorance in each other's emotional keyboards, his / her level of general intelligence,and the lack of the **PSYCHOLOGICAL INTELLIGENCE** are accountable in each unhappy family case, each devorce , or a ruined relationship. In China, by the way, women and men are *more family-oriented,* and they treat sexual digressions of a man or a woman with understanding and even respect, *preserving the love climate for the children in a family*. The man provides for the family and displays love and care for the children.

The sanctity of a family must the Law in our lives!

The seeds of pure, sincere feelings have been planted in us by our much more romantically minded ancesters. **It's our responsibility to nurture them** now with new Self-Love and Self-Awareness that demand holisic parameters (*physical, emotiona,mental,spiritual, universal*) in making the chioce of a love parner. **Let's not stereotype people by their sex preferences!** Let everyone decide for themselves who and why they chose as a partner in this very challenging life. I have noted above that the level of a *person's self-consciousness* is what should bother us. **The rest is God's domain!**Our new, digitally enhanced **CULTURE OF LIFE** demands a new personality **ACCULTURATION** *(See Part One above)*, based on new knowledge, deeper phicological awareness, and a much wider perception of the social and cultural reality.in its five basic strata. **Love is the unity of all of them.**

Love-Worth is a Very Fragile Force!

4. Let's Display No Negligence to Emotional Intelligence!

In sum, in the emotional management plane, <u>it's vital to be free from self-blame!</u> Try to forgive yourself for being sometimes weak, fearful, and indecisive. If you are a good, kind, and noble person, you are already worthy of celebrating yourself! Also, <u>forgive others for their indiscretions</u> . It's only then that the justification" *No one is perfect!* works.

Put the past part of your life behind you. Feel free of the hurt and harm done to you, Without the emotional burden of unforgetting and unforgiving, you will be lighter and free to fly, while the other person will have to live with the unfair deed done to you for the rest of his / her life. *Lack of Emotional Diplomacy* in a relationship is a projection of our life on the global international plane. Emotional Diplomacy must also be the core <u>in the International Diplomacy Store!</u>

Deficiency in emotional diplomacy skills and therefore, <u>lack of international sanity and peace gravity</u> in the heads of many world leaders causes conflicts, territorial pretensions, threats of war, and all kinds of political discords that just seek more power, but in fact, display a low self-worth and self-consciousness.

A self-exceptional leader always has <u>diplomatic patience</u> and will stand for the will of his people for peace, understanding, mutual respect, and the recognition of the boarders of another country because *our main evolutionary global goal on Earth* must be the **RIGHT FOR LIFE** and the opportunity to prove our self-worth in it. But in most cases the world leaders care less for the people that granted them power.

The mind-se below must become *a world-wide international law* that would guarantee peace, love, and worldwide stability.

The Sense of Measure is Love Treasure!

5. Have No Strife in Your Emotional Life!

The Reminder: Having completed **the Emotional level** of reviewing *"Self-Renaissance"* essential standpoints, don't forget to conduct **SELF-SCANNING,** following the evolutionary paradigm

Self-Synthesis ➡ **Self-Analysis** ➡ *Self-Synthesis!*

(Self-Awareness) ➡ *(Self-Monitoring + Self-Installation + Self-Realization)* ➡ *(Self-Salvation)*

Self-Synthesis starts with making up the **HOLISTIC PICTURE OF SELF** every day , *doing it most objectively ,consciously, and honestly.*

Self-Analysis must be conducted as a quick review of your *physical, emotional, mental, spiritual, and universal* realms of life. This **SELF X-RAYING** will show you what strata of life you succeed in or fail .

Analyze 1) *your health* and the physical activity. **2)** *the attitude to yourself* and the people around you, **3)** *new knowledge* that you enriched your intelligence with and the strategic plan of action, leading to your full professional self-realization, 4) *your faith* and following its messages in action. *5) commitment to your exceptionality,* your goal in life. Don't ever betray your self-worth!

Final Self-Synthesis – Completing the **SELF-ASSESSMENT,** give yourself grades for each level separately and figure out the average grade for the day, on your own scale - *(3.5 /,4, 6 etc.)* You must assess the *ability to manage yourself in the time and space of the reality.*

Your **"SUPER I"** must be constantly self-assessed! Self-scanning, as a general, objective vision of Self, is very beneficial if you visualize the paradigm of self-creation all the time. *Vision helps in Self- Renaissance coding precision!* Know your way; don't sway!

Your Body is the Temple, Your Mind is the Priest! Don't Role Twist!

Tough Times Do Not Last, Tough Beings Do!

(Best Photos - Internet Collection)

"Hitch Your Wagon to a Star!"

(R.W.Emerson -"Society and Solitude")

<u>Stage One</u>

(Self-Monitored Stage for a Self-Renaissance Sage)

Physical Dimension - Self-Awareness

Sustainability

is Our

<u>Main Life Ability!</u>

(Rule # 55 of Self-Renaissance)

The Way You Use Your Life is Your Own Design. <u>So, Don't Whine!</u>

Self-Culture Means Holistically Based Self-Acculturation!

Emotional

Form   +   Content

(Body+ Spirit+ Mind) + (Self-Consciousness + Universal Consciousness)

Living Intelligence   +   Enlightened Self-Consciousness = A Whole Self!

Diplomacy

5. Universal Realm = Self- Acculturated;

4. Spiritual Realm = Self- Realized!

3. Mental Realm = Self-Educated;

2. Emotional Realm = Self-Controlled;

1. Physical Realm = Self-Aware

The Harmony of the Heart + Mind Sync is the Main Goal of the Emotional + Mental link = Personal Gravity = Self-Consciousness

The process of raising Self-Consciousness is very complicated and must be consciously monitored by everyone of us, willing to upgrade their physical, emotional, mental, spiritual, and universal status in life.

Self-Consciousness Formation is the New Form of

Self-Acculturation!

Section 1

Self-Renaissance and Physical Mangement

Synchronize Your Life's Base with the Nature's Beautiful Haze!

Take care of " the hardness in the body, sharpness in the mind ,

and softness in the heart!" (Sadhguru)

Be Exceptional at that!

See Your Physical Sustainability as the Universal Life Infinity!

1. Practice What I Preach!

The physical realm of life is pretty developed now, but you need to continue working on your **phisical status in unity** with the *emotional, mental, spiritual, and universal* circles of your life. The present-day technological times have changed *the gravitational force* of both men and women. The essential role of a woman to be a wife and a mother is enriched now with being a good professional, a manager, a CEO, or even the owner of a big company .Men, in turn, do not depend on women to cook for them and take care of all their needs. Life and technology have utilized many of our needs, having changed the **gravitational value** of a family and a committed relationship. Technology has freed space in our brains and hearts *to liberate and enhance our intelligence exceptionality guts!* If in old times, our life struggle was limited by the fight for existence, **it is characterized now with a personality's expression persistence**!

A personable man has an individuality of an exceptional personality. *Exceptionality of a person, a man or a woman, attracts more than sex appeal!*. Many people now seek different ways to stand out and attract attention to their individualities- piecing their faces, using content-based tattoos, getting uncommonly dressed, etc. But the physical level of self-expression is not enough now. **We must be exceptional in all of them!** *For instance*, one of the most beautiful women of the world, a very educated woman, the mother of four kids, *the Queen of Jordan, Rania Yassin* writes, *"Let's judge women now by what they have in their heads, not on their heads."* Women have a more acute intuition and establish the **mind + heart link** much easier than men, inviting them to follow suit. This sacredly instilled in us connection changes the world and helps us accumulate personal gravity, magnetism, and charisma.

Emotional Gravity Generates Personal Magnetism!

2. We're Fit for Life only with the Holistic Order Inside!

Keep the holistic paradigm in the mind's vision and follow the structure to create the Self-Renaissance **OPERATIONAL SYSTEM** in yourself. It must be based on ***Personal Gravity and the Emotional Diplomacy Skill*** so you could rightfully declare: **I Know who I Am**, and **I know who I'm Not!** Women are much more evolved now, and the frailness of relationships is often connected with men getting into a competition with women in the professional and private lives.

My own first marriage fell apart because my self-realization plans were not shared by my husband. The physical level of our life is the basic one because the body is your operational system, and the mind is its operator. **The mind and the heart in sync do the trick!** So, keep enacting the new life paradigm,

I am a strong, calm, and determined owner of my firm will.

I can *operate my life successfully!.*

I want to *operate my life very successfully!.*

And I will *operate my life.most sucessfully!*

I'm becoming better and better at it with each breath. I love my life's Quest!

I remind you to do the **SELF-SCANNING** daily as **the self-refining training of your Self-Renaissance Operational System**., following the paradigm - ***Synthesis -Analysis -Synthesis.*** Consistency, even a sporadic one, will bring you to **the inner equillibrium.** This simple auto-suggestive action plugs your body into the energy system of the Sun and the Universal Informational Field. The more light you generate inside, the stronger your **SOLAR SYSTEM** is!

Choreograph Your Self-Renaissance Dance, Always, Not Once!

3. Self-Awareness and Self-Gravity in Sync Do the Trick!

I am tolerant and patient,

I am mindful and sensational!

I am moved by the inner steel

Of my determination will!

I am immune to depression,

Anger, hate, and aggression!

I am not perfect, yet,

But I am on my way to the Best of Me array!

For a man or a woman of action,

I am an irresistible attraction!

Everyone can perceive

The positive vibes that they receive!

The vibes that inspire

To act and to rewire,

The vibes that make things doable

And a dull spirit re- movable!

I'm Kind to the Unkind. I'm One of a Kind!

(Rule # 56 of Emotional Diplomacy)

Long Live the Belief in Myself Without "IF!"

4. Stop Being a Human Ant!

Disconnectedness in the fractal unity is the **MIND - BODY** destruction. So, it's vital to get into the habit of *X-raying yourself holistically in five dimensions* before falling asleep. Having assessed yourself in the physical realm of life, do the self-scanning of your emotional life and admit if you hurt anybody's feelings. Be sure to apologize to that person then and there, in person or over the phone. Be sure to forgive someone if there was an apology. **Keep radiating light from inside!**

Be aware of the spectrum of each life's momentum!

Next, praise yourself if you have learnt, read, heard something interesting that day to enrich your mental outlay. Also, pray with the *sincerest attitude of gratitude* for the progress that you've made in your self-growth in the spiritual realm. (*See the Reminder page*). Conclude your self-scanning admitting that you remain true to your universal goal in life that must always be based on *the exceptionality of your personality,* not on your material accomplishments that are just the side dish on the Self-Realization plate of your self-monitored fate.

It's like simulator training in technology.

Thus, you'll develop a joyful, forgiving, and energy refilling gut in sync with the energy of your rising self-consciousness in every level. Unless we take care of raising self-consciousness, we'll have to exclaim like William Shakespeare, *"Oh, people! From dirt you came and to dirt you remain!"*But if knowledge is constantly refreshed and self-acculturation is in your **AWARE ATTENTION LOOP**, you'll start *sub-consciously recognizing the holistic paradigm* within the structure of your thoughts. Structuring your thoughts consciously, you'll end up saying precisely what you mean and doing what you've strategized. That's a huge victory!

You are Becoming an Integral Fractal of Life!

5. Economize Energy for Your Human Machine in Every Gene!

In order to obtain *a permanent connection between the higher and lower levels of Self*, you need <u>to reduce fractal tension</u> at every stage of your Being with the help of *the Active and Passive Meditation.(See Part Two above)*

Learn to relax in the entire body mass in one cycle of the spiral, not once!

(Body + Spirit + Mind) + (Self-Consciousness + Universal Consciousness)

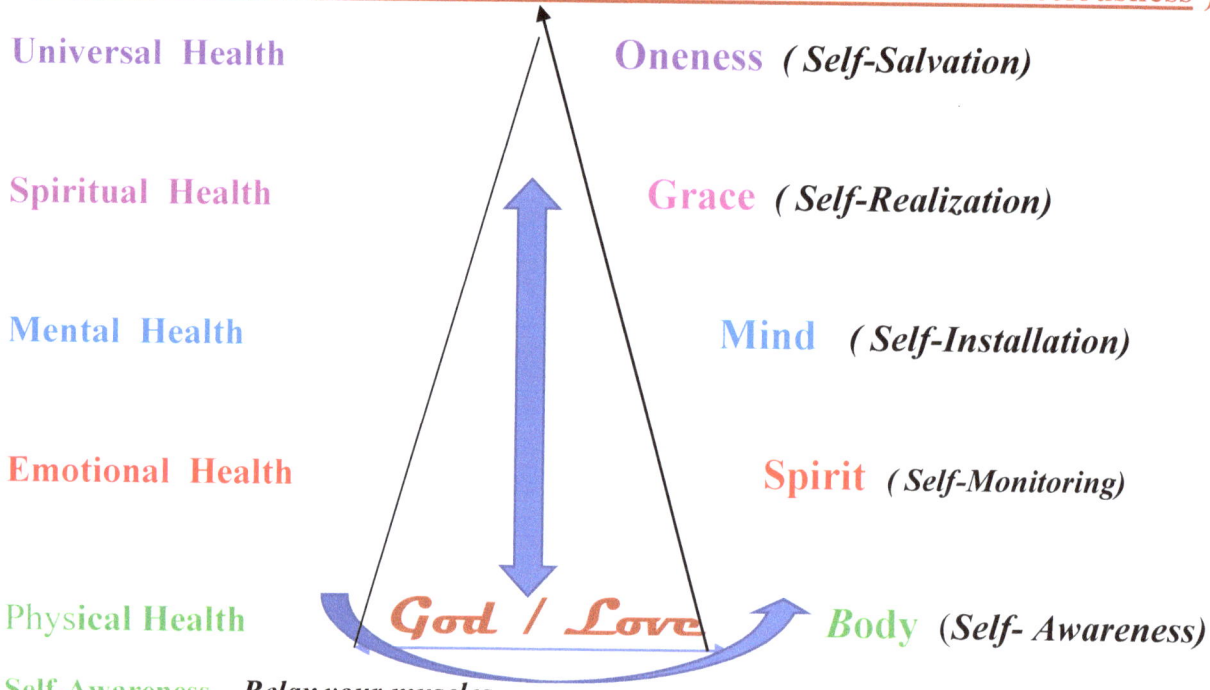

Universal Health	**Oneness** *(Self-Salvation)*
Spiritual Health	**Grace** *(Self-Realization)*
Mental Health	**Mind** *(Self-Installation)*
Emotional Health	**Spirit** *(Self-Monitoring)*
Physical Health	**God / Love** **Body** *(Self- Awareness)*

Self-Awareness – *Relax your muscles.*

Self-Monitoring – *Relax the inner emotional tension, and the tension of the tongue.*

Self- Installation - *Relax your mind and fill it up with infinity.* Self-acceptance is as important as self-improvement now

Self-Realization – *Relax your faith and embrace the world in its width..*

Self- Salvation - *Relax the entire Self and fill every cell up with infinity!* Conclude the relaxation with Self-Elation and the mindset installation!

I'm Unique in Every Stance; I was born but only Once. There wasn't, there isn't, there won't Ever be Anyone like Me!

6. Stick to the New Life Paradigm!

In sum, Self-Renaissance <u>in the physical sense</u> is erecting the temple of the body's *physical, emotional ,mental spiritual, and universal stems* holistically remembering about all the other levels of self-perfection. We are all mortal. We are aware of that, but *we forget about* it when we get drunk, drugged out, or angry. **Life with lack of Emotional Diplomacy Skills becomes a fallacy!**

But if you are <u>Self-Renaissance-oriented,</u> you generate goodness, kindness, joy and happiness in every dimension of your life and around you for the people who share your space and time. The main source of energy on the Earth is the Sun, and the lighter you are inside, the stronger your own solar system is. <u>**Personal magnetism is at its core, and people gravitate to you more!**</u>

 If your mind is constantly set for self-improvement, your <u>self-consciousness will be mushrooming.</u> You will always feel good about your *joy-generating life*. Interestingly, the scientists of *the George Washington University* prove in their research that a person who has <u>a much higher self-consciousness,</u> not just wisdom that old people normally have, enjoys life and living more because *he has the purpose to make himself better*, and it changes his perception of life entirely.

<u>Self-Renaissance is making its beauty dance!</u>

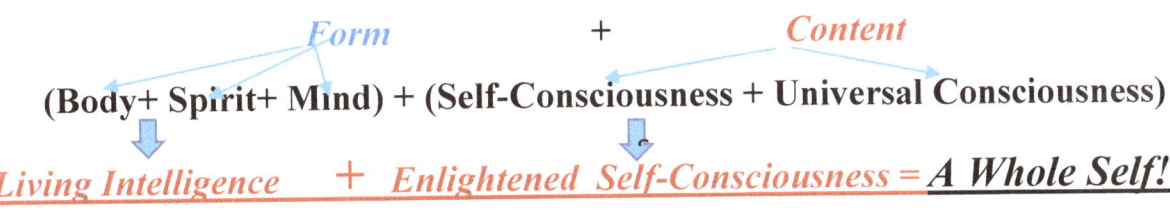

Form + *Content*

(Body+ Spirit+ Mind) + (Self-Consciousness + Universal Consciousness)

Living Intelligence + *Enlightened Self-Consciousness = A Whole Self!*

In the Bank of God's Account, Deposit Personal Gravity and Steady Morality, not Indifference, Anger, and Frugality!

7. Have Fun with Your Inner Sun!

When you wake up in the morning and look at yourself in the mirror, be sure *to induct yourself with youth, health , and a great mood*. Check my **Panegyric to Life** at the beginning of this book and sing it in yourself! You are a life's unique cell !So, keep reminding to yourself:

I'm 27 (37, 47,….)

And Not a Day More!

I'm as Young as Ever Before!

I'm Dynamic, as Ever;

I'm Sluggish – Never!

I was, I am, and I will be Young

Forever!

(Rule # 57 of Self-Renaissance)

To Be Inspired, Be Self-Inspiring!

8. Self-Renaissance Cones of Dos and Don'ts!

+ Dos

1. The Universal Realm – <u>Self-Salvation</u> - *Know thyself at each level and in every dimension!* You radiate what you emanate! *Your exceptionality must be devoid of greed, indifference and vanity.*

2. The Spiritual Realm – <u>Self - Realization</u> - *Put your spiritual maturation in sync with the God's link. Acquire spiritual intelligence without dogmatic negligence*

3. The Mental Realm- <u>Self-Installation</u>-" *There's only One God - knowledge and One evil - ignorance.* " *(Socrates) Keep sifting the information to become a wiser Self-Actualizer.*

4. The Emotional Realm – <u>Self-Monitoring</u> – *Make Your Heart Smart and your mind -kind. Be One of a kind! The mind + heart link must be always in in sync!*

5. The Physical Realm- <u>Self-Awareness</u> – *Take charge of your internal pharmacy! Conduct a self-restriction war.-* <u>Less is More!</u>

- Don'ts

1. *The Physical Realm -* <u>Self-Awareness</u> - *Don't be a slave of Self.* Don't destroy yourself! *Your self-emancipation is the salvation!*

2. *The Emotional Realm -* <u>Self- Monitoring</u> – *Don't mix your personal might with the poison of life!* Don't rust from lust! *Love that is betrayed has no rebate!*

3. *The Mental Realm -* <u>Self-Installation</u> – *Not to ever fall, you need to Self-Install! Don't let your intelligence stagnation kill your life's elation!*

4. *The Spiritual Realm –* <u>Self-Realization</u> - *Conscience counselling shouldn't be bouncing! Don't leave your soul without any control!*

5. *The Universal Realm –* <u>Self-Salvation</u> - *Don't betray your life's unique exceptionality for the life's banality! Don't crawl - fly!*

Self-Progress or Self-Regress is Your Life's Process!

9. Conclude Your Journey in the Physical Dimension with Elation!

The Reminder: Having completed **the Physical level** of reviewing the essential standpoints of Self-Renaissance, I complete the book structure, following the design of the DNA figure **8.** *(See Book Rationale, 7)*

Self-Synthesis ➡️ **Self-Analysis** ➡️ *Self-Synthesis!*

(Self-Awareness) ➡️ *(Self-Monitoring + Self-Installation +Self-Realization)* ➡️ **(Self-Salvation)**

Self-Synthesis starts with making up the **HOLISTIC PICTURE OF SELF** every day , doing it most objectively ,consciously, and honestly.

Self-Analysis must be conducted as a quick review of your *physical, emotional, mental, spiritual, and universal* realms of life. This **SELF X-RAYING** will show you what strata of life you succeed in or fail .

Analyze 1**)** *your health* and the physical activity**. 2)** *the attitude to yourself* and the people around you, **3)** *new knowledge* that you enriched your intelligence with and the strategic plan of action, leading to your full professional self-realization, 4) *your faith* and following its messages in action**.** **5)** *commitment to your exceptionality,* your goal in life. Don't ever betray your self-worth!

Final Self-Synthesis – Completing the **SELF-ASSESSMENT** in five levels **,** give yourself **the average grade** for having reasoned out the standpoints of this book. In other words, you must assess the ability to manage yourself better now. Your **"SUPER I"** must be constantly self-assessed all your life, and I wish you success on this path.

Be Whole. Stop stumbling in the dark of Your Soul!

The Greatest Energy Remains to Be the Energy of the Unbeatable Spirit of Thee!

The Sunset is the Sign of the Sunrise in a Holistic Twine!

(Winston Churchill)

Make Every Age of Yours the Reflection of the Sunrise-Sunset Vintage!

Internalize the Emotions but Externalize the Mind.

Be One of a Kind!

Everything good takes time, willpower, and a good mood!

(Rule # 58 of Self-Renaissance)

"Life is the Love Romance with Yourself."(Oscar Wilde)

1. Put the Form + Content of Your Life in Sync; Feel but Think!

Finally, thanks to consciously and consistently conducted self-scanning and inspirational self-boosting, the inner chaos that you might be experiencing at one time or another will gradually turn to the constructive order in the *physical, emotional, mental, spiritual, and universal* realms of your life. A great French writer, *Antoine de Saint-Exupery* wrote in his very insightful book" *The Little Prince,"*

"It's only by judging ourselves that we can grow as individuals."

When the process of self-growth is willful and constantly reasoned out, we are at peace with ourselves, and we are more pleasant to deal with for other people. That's why when we do good things, we feel balanced and content. In fact, we become godly. *"Our consciousness is a chaotic informational phenomenon, based on the processes of order."* (*Dmitriy Vereshchagin*) The order is obtained with the thought and tongue control, focused on the electromagnetic unity of the heart and the mind.

An exceptionally knowledgeable esoteric researcher, the founder of the *School of Remembering"* *Drunvalo Melchizedek* in his very informing book *"The Flower of Life "* explains to us *the sacred geometry of life* and the formation of the center of our being - **MERKABAH.**

Drunvalo Melchizedek presents a bigger picture of life and helps us see ourselves as being interconnected to the Universe or all forms of life by cultivating *the unity of the left-right polarized magnetic charges in the heart* and finding the spot of their sacred connection, *the zero concentration of energy,* our inner equilibrium. With this image in the mind, the essence of any meditation takes a clear-cut meaning because the heart's inner unity translates to the left-right brains' unity and, thus, to the entire body and its self-consciousness equanimity.

Be Wise! Synthesize Your Soul's Size!

2. Self-Consciousness Accumulation

A Refined Soul must be in Your Full Control!

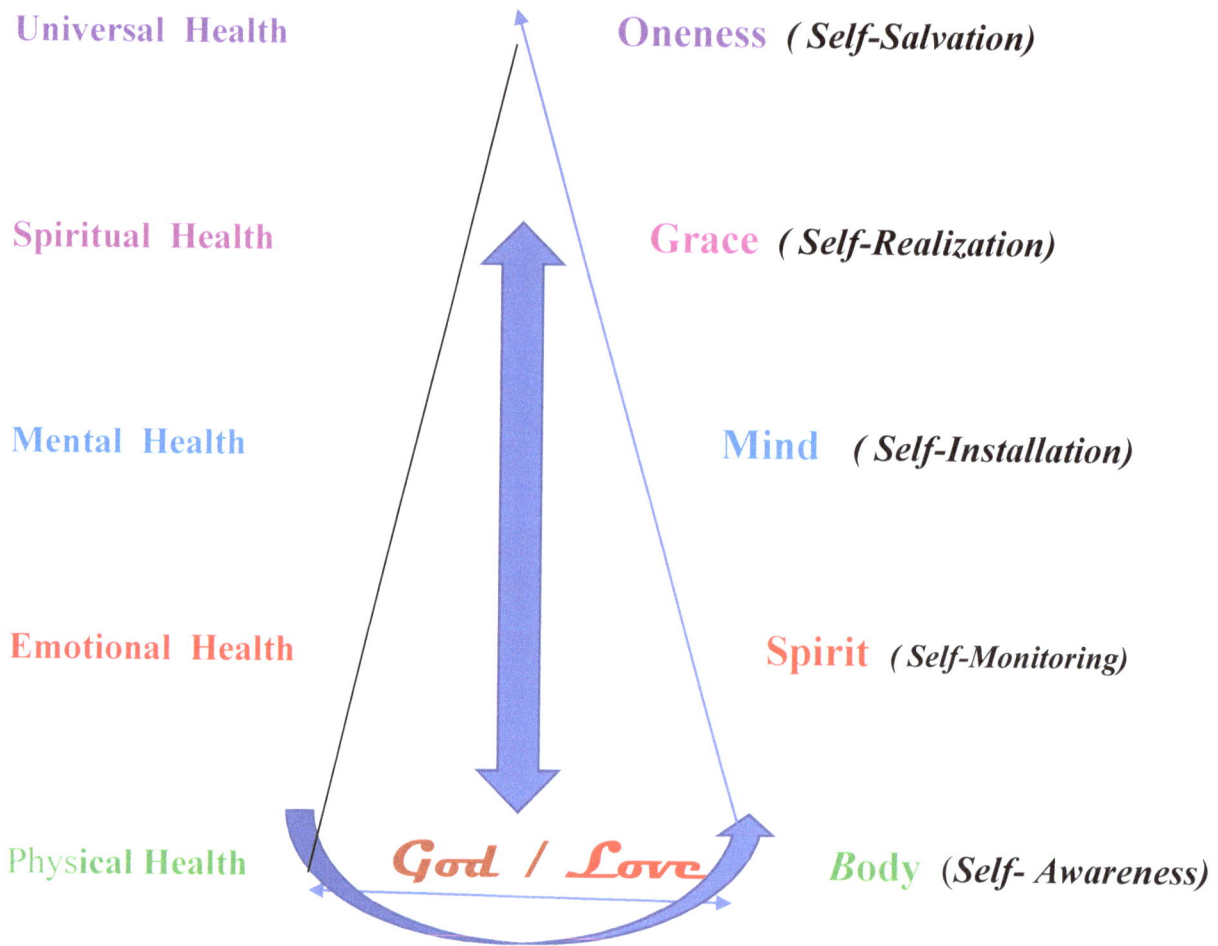

Universal Health   Oneness *(Self-Salvation)*

Spiritual Health   Grace *(Self-Realization)*

Mental Health   Mind *(Self-Installation)*

Emotional Health   Spirit *(Self-Monitoring)*

Physical Health   *God / Love*   Body *(Self- Awareness)*

(Body+ Spirit+ Mind + Self-Consciousness + Universal Consciousness)

On the path of Self-Renaissance, don't allow yourself to stay broken, upset, irritated, disappointed, old, unloved, or depressed.

(Rule # 59 of Self-Renaissance)

Life is Not Years on Your Calendar; It's the Result of Your Self-Consciousness Accumulation without Any Frustration!

3. Self-Renaissance Skills at Play Today!

In sum, I hope that the **Paradigm of Self-Renaissance** presented here will help you establish a holistic unity in the *physical, emotional, mental, spiritual, and universal* realms of life. This unity is governed by the fractal connection of the form and content of your life that must also be based on **love** and **self-worth**. Working on the heart + mind **SYNEGISTIC UNITY,** you are perfecting not just the body, but the spirit and, most importantly, *your self-consciousness*. This last book in the series of seven others makes up the Inspirational Psychology for Self-Ecology that can always be enriched with the new information, retaining the objectivity of its system.

Thus, you will be focusing on *the qualities of Self-Renaissance* at every stage of self-growth. 1. Self-Awareness *(physical dimension)*; **2.** Self-Monitoring *(emotional dimension)*; **3.** Self-Installation (*mental dimension)*; **4.** Self-Realization *(spiritual dimension , and* **5.** Self-Salvation (*universal dimension)*.

Self-Ecology + Love Ecology + Self-Worth + Self-Renaissance =

= AN ACCULTURATED PERSONALITY!

So, keep developing the Emotional Diplomacy Skills and have a *clear-cut vision of the blueprint of the plan of action* in your mind. In a nutshell,.

1) Respect your own and other people's individuality (*physical dimension),*

2) Learn the peculiarities of operating your own and the people of your space and time emotional keyboard *(emotional dimension),*

3) Enrich consistently your mental outlook and the scope of your *professional awareness. (mental dimension),*

4) Treat with reverence your own and other people's spiritual values (*spiritual dimension),*

5) And finally, acknowledge your universal gift, your *exceptionality* that translates into your peculiar mission on the planet Earth .*(Universal dimension)*

Life is Brief, but It's Still the Best Gift!

4. Nothing is Impossible if You Make Your Self-Renaissance Irreversible!

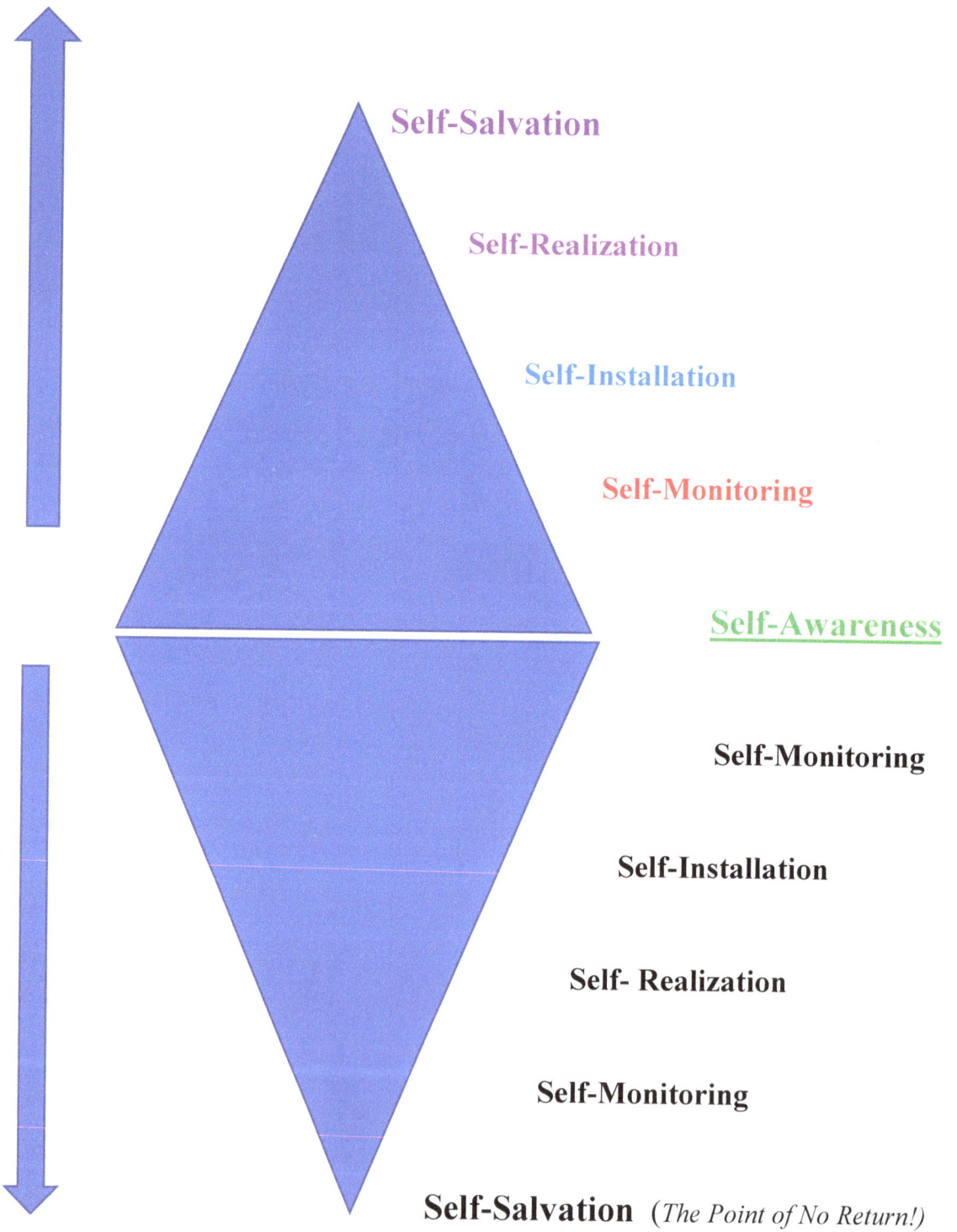

Self-Salvation

Self-Realization

Self-Installation

Self-Monitoring

Self-Awareness

Self-Monitoring

Self-Installation

Self- Realization

Self-Monitoring

Self-Salvation *(The Point of No Return!)*

Your Life is Becoming and Zooming

5. Self-Emancipation is in Self-Crystallization!

In conclusion, the final **SELF-SYNTHESIS** of our reviewing *Self-Renaissance* in five circles of life is the basic one and the most challenging to attain because our physical being is constantly and holistically overseen by the Universal Intelligence, enveloping us from inside out *in an integral unity of the Oneness of life.* According to *Deepak Chopra,*

"When our life is whole, we become holy!"

Not to go down the road of self-corrode, we should never allow the evil forces in us and around you to destroy the system of self-creation that we have sought to pursue. To evoke the struggle between **"YES and NO" scales of life , making sacrifice** sacrifice is necessary because if nothing is sacrificed, nothing is obtained.

The " **SIMPLEXITY"** of the paradigm , the simple and complex in a fix, and *self-observation* must become the solid new habit with you, without which Self-Renaissance is not possible to be ever attained. *Inner simplicity and naturalness, honesty and sincerity with oneself are* the first requirement of our life-governing cells! So, follow the guidelines, inducting yourself with:

My gestures are mild; my smile is kind.

My touch is nice; my words are wise!

My support is strong; my generosity is far gone!

Love is my action; Patience is my reaction!

Precision is my talking; pride is my walking!

I Work More on Your Self-Renaissance Core!

6. Let's Expand Our Universal Consciousness Stand!

The Universal Informational Field has its own planetary currents that merge in the *Global Informational Memory Storage*. We need to learn "to do shopping" in it with the benefit for many, for all, for the world at large.

Learning to form ourselves, we are learning *to shape the Informational Field* around us. It gets in sync with the Universal Laws and, in this process, we are heightening the level of our vibrations and, therefore, our *Self-Consciousness* and *Self-Renaissance!*

(Rule # 60 of Self-Renaissance)

Life is Going on,
And It's Great in Our Godly Form!

7. Self-Renaissance is the Action of Looking into the Mirror of Your Soul!

Let Your Self-Resurrection be Perfect in Reflection!

Dr. Ray with Her Inspirational Say!

1. *"Emotional Diplomacy or Follow the Bliss of the Uncatchable Is!"/ Editorial* LEIRIS, New York, USA,2005, 2010

2. *"Five Dimensions of the Soul"* / in Russian, LEIRIS Publishing, New York, USA, 2011

3. *"Americanize Your Language, Emotionalize Your Speech!"* / Nova Press, USA, 2011

4. *"It Too Shall Pass!"* (Inspirational Boosters in Five Dimensions) / Xlibris, 2012- **Second Edition – by Workbook Press -2020**

5. *"I am Strong in My Spirit!"* (Inspirational Boosters in Russian) / Xlibris, 2013.

6. *"Language Intelligence or Universal English"* (Method of the Right Language Behavior), **Book One** /Xlibris, 2013 – **Second edition- , Stonewallpress,2019**

7. *"Language Intelligence or Universal English"* (Remedy Your Language Habits," **Book Two** /Xlibris, 2013 – Also, Stonewallpress,2019

8. *"Language Intelligence or Universal English,"* (Remedy Your Speech Skills) **Book Three** /Xlibris, 2013- Also, Stonewallpress,2019

9. *"My Solar System,"* (Auto-Suggestive Psychology for Inner Ecology) Xlibris, 2015 /republished – **Second Edition by UR Link Print and Media, 2020**

The Books on Self-Resurrection in five life dimensions:

10. *"I Am Free to Be the Best of Me!"*- (Physical Dimension) - Toplinkpublishing.com. Sept. 2017) – Second Edition , Book Whip, 2019- **Second Edition**

11. *Soul-Refining!* (Emotional Dimension) (Toplinkpublishing.com. May 2017) - **Second Edition by Global Summit House, 2020**

12. *"Living Intelligence or the Art of Becoming!"*(Mental Dimension)- Xlibris, 2015 – Second Edition (Bookwhip,2019-**Third Edition- by Global Summit House, 2020 / Excellence Book Award, 2020**

13. *"Self-Taming"* (Life-Gaining is in Self-Taming!)(Spiritual Dimension)- Book Whip, 2019- **Second Edition by Global Summit House, 2020**

14. *" Beyond the Terrestrial!"* (Be the Station for Self-Inspiration!) - (Universal Dimension) /-, First Edition-Xlibris, 2016./ Second Edition Book Whip, 2018 Third Edition - **URLink Print and Media, 2019**

15. *'"The State of Love from the Above!"*- **Book Whip, 2018**

259

16. "*Love Ecology*"- **Dr. Rimaletta Ray Publishing., 2020**

17. "*Self-Worth* "- **Dr. Rimaletta Ray Publishing , 2020**

www. Language – fitness.com / *Trailer -Section* "**Self-Resurrection**"

email - dr.rimaletta@gmail.com **Tel. (203) 212-2673**

Self-Renaissance is Me;

Self-Renaissance is My Philosophy!

The pictures, **conceptually illustrating the messages of the book, are from my Internet collection – "Best Photos."** *I admire a rare talent of the unknown photographers and their peculiar vision of the beauty of the world.*

I thank all the contributors of pictures in this book wholeheartedly *for the honor of using these pieces of real craftsmanship for our common inspiration with life and living.*

The pictures on the cover and the last page by Natalia Shenkova / aszh@rambler.ru

----

Thank You All

for Sharing with Me

Some of Thee!

www.ingramcontent.com/pod-product-compliance
Lightning Source LLC
Chambersburg PA
CBHW041112120626
46547CB00019B/2678